T0357062

IMAGES
of America

LGBTQ DENVER

MASTER OF THE MAIN STAGE. DeMarcio Slaughter, pictured here in 2016, first emceed a drag performance on PrideFest's Center Stage in 2003 and, within three years, became the event's chief entertainment coordinator and emcee, bringing in celebrity entertainers and *RuPaul's Drag Race* contestants. Slaughter helped grow PrideFest attendance into the hundreds of thousands with a volunteer team that annually showcases local talent as well as national headliners. "I do this work to make a positive impact on younger audiences, while still entertaining those who have been hanging with me and Center Stage for over two decades," says Slaughter. (Photograph by Stevie Crecelius.)

ON THE COVER: In its fifth year, Denver's 1981 Pride parade swelled to a couple thousand participants proceeding from Cheesman Park along East Colfax Avenue to Civic Center Park. In earlier years, the event alternated between a celebration with floats and costumes and more politically charged marches demanding rights and justice. "Gay Freedom Week of 1981 took on a more political vibe," wrote History Colorado's Aaron Marcus, "with speakers . . . claiming that no sympathetic city councilperson or state representative or senator would champion legislation specifically protecting gays." That would begin to change during the coming decade. (Photograph by Phil Nash.)

IMAGES
of America

LGBTQ DENVER

Phil Nash
Foreword by Dr. Tom Noel

ARCADIA
PUBLISHING

Copyright © 2024 by Phil Nash
ISBN 978-1-4671-6118-3

Published by Arcadia Publishing
Charleston, South Carolina

Printed in the United States of America

Library of Congress Control Number: 2023950411

For all general information, please contact Arcadia Publishing:
Telephone 843-853-2070
Fax 843-853-0044
E-mail sales@arcadiapublishing.com

Visit us on the Internet at www.arcadiapublishing.com

*Dedicated to the multitudes of courageous LGBTQ
volunteers and allies for their time, treasure, expertise, and
passion to shape a more just and humane society*

CONTENTS

FOREWORD

Between 1972 and 1976, I studied Denver's early gay bar scene, leading to the first published history of Denver's LGBTQ community. Back then, Denver police were harassing gays. In response, the gay community began organizing. Working with historian colleague Terry Mangan, a cofounder of the Gay Coalition of Denver, I witnessed Denver's earliest post-Stonewall stirrings of gay activism. Early successes sparked a chain of events, eventually drawing tens of thousands of Denverites out of the closet. Over time, they have built a vibrant LGBTQ culture helping make Denver one of the nation's most desirable cities.

Rarely is history written by people who made it. It is usually scholars who shape fragments of evidence, like puzzle pieces, to shape a narrative of the past. Phil Nash, *LGBTQ Denver*'s author, has both participated in and witnessed Denver's LGBTQ history. I first met Phil in the late 1970s shortly after he became the first director of the Denver-based Gay Community Center of Colorado, today known as the Center on Colfax. In the 1980s, as a journalist, Phil reported on the LGBTQ community as it faced the AIDS epidemic as well as opportunities afforded by a more inclusive political landscape. When an antigay backlash developed in the early 1990s with Colorado's Amendment 2 banning state and local government from enacting gay rights, the *Denver Post* featured Phil's guest editorials denouncing the discrimination. In his professional career with Denver city government, foundations, and nonprofit organizations, Phil informed policies and practices to ensure that the LGBTQ community could be seen, heard, and included. Phil tells me he dislikes the word "retirement," and though he no longer receives a paycheck, he still has a mission. Part of it is publishing this book to help younger generations of LGBTQ people, their allies, historians, and others understand the remarkable evolution of Denver's LGBTQ community.

LGBTQ Denver is the first thorough history of Denver's LGBTQ community. It should interest all Coloradans. How we treat LGBTQ people signifies our broader tolerance for diverse groups. After watching the liberation struggles of Chicanos, Blacks, women, and Asians, LGBTQ people have gradually organized and won their civil rights. Today all groups, straight and gay, join hands to celebrate Pride every June. It's been a long journey along a difficult road. We are blessed to have someone who was there for most of it now telling the story in these pages.

—Tom "Dr. Colorado" Noel

ACKNOWLEDGMENTS

One of the biggest challenges in documenting LGBTQ pictorial history is that so much of it remains in the basements, attics, scrapbooks, and storage boxes of private individuals and electronic data files of organizations. As I contacted many of these individuals for specific kinds of images they might have, I soon realized I wasn't just asking for a particular photograph, I was also asking that individual to spend hours locating the photograph, scanning it to high-resolution specifications, and transmitting it to me—and sometimes redoing scans if they were low-quality. Thanks to the following people for helping me with this project: Sue Anderson, Annie Brenman-West, Nadine Bridges, Judge Mary Celeste (Ret.), Brad Clark, David Ford, Gillian Ford, Rex Fuller, Kevin Gardner, Janet Gilmore, Robin Kniech, Christi Layne (Christopher Sloan), Monica Lloyd, Kevin Malloy, Debra Pollock, Morris Price, Chris Seymour, Robert Steele, Darrell Watson, and David Westman.

I am deeply grateful to David Duffield, director of the LGBTQ History Project at the Center on Colfax, and to Aaron Marcus, Gill Foundation Associate Curator of LGBTQ+ History at History Colorado, for their unconditional support for this endeavor by sharing images, researching sources, and providing expert input on the accuracy of the book's written narrative. I have relied heavily on Bill Olson's sharp memory and his treasure trove of images and documentation dating back to the 1960s. Gerald Gerash's meticulous documentation of the political strides made during the early 1970s has been invaluable, as are David Ford's images of events in the 1980s and early 1990s and Mary Celeste's images documenting the overturning of Amendment 2 in the mid-1990s.

Several organizations have been especially helpful in furnishing images and information and making staff available to support my work. Many thanks to the Center on Colfax (lgbtqcolorado.org), the Gill Foundation (gillfoundation.org), History Colorado (historycolorado.org), and One Colorado (one-colorado.org). Photographers who were contracted by these organizations are credited if they are known. Those photographers include Stevie Creselius, Eric Holladay-McCann, T.J. Romero, and Evan Semón.

Thanks to several online sources, I was able to find images representing a broader diversity of the community's history. I am grateful to the Library of Congress, Visit Denver, and several photographers who granted permission to use images they made.

It has been my intent to recognize everyone who has directly or indirectly contributed to *LGBTQ Denver*. I apologize for any unintended omissions or errors.

INTRODUCTION

Denver is the largest city for at least 600 miles in any direction. You have to go to Chicago, Dallas, Phoenix, or even Kansas City to come close. Denver is globally connected with one of the busiest airports in the world. As an all-direction transportation hub for the Western United States, its reputation for outdoor recreation, healthy lifestyles, and a thriving economy attracts thousands of new residents each year. While the Rocky Mountain West is generally politically and socially conservative, Denver is the progressive hub of a blue state that elected the first openly gay governor in the nation and where LGBTQ elected officials, media personalities, business executives, professionals, artists, and civic leaders are able to be open, visible, and vocal. As of 2023, Colorado scores 42.5 out of a possible 43.5 for its LGBTQ-friendly policies according to the Movement Advancement Project. Denver's annual Pride celebration is one of the five largest in the nation.

It hasn't always been this way. Homosexual behavior was against the law almost from Denver's founding in 1858. Sodomy, defined in territorial law as "the infamous crime against nature either with man or beast," (heterosexual or homosexual) was outlawed in 1861 when Colorado was still a territory. (Decades later, courts defined sodomy to include oral sex.) Such laws were standard fare, rooted in colonial Puritanism as white settlers moved west. In early Denver, there were no definitions categorizing people as straight, gay, bi, transgender, or other identities recognized today. In male homosocial clusters, such as mining camps, ranches, and military installations, same-sex relations were prevalent and not stigmatized. Sodomy laws were rarely enforced and usually only on aggressors when sex was coerced. Female impersonators, for entertainment or sex work, appeared in Denver as early as the 1870s. Some women lived and dressed as men to get paid work. Scholars have uncovered Denver homosexual gathering places from as early as the 1880s mixed in with the commercialized sex district located around Eighteenth Street near Larimer and Market Streets. Recent analyses of census data from the late 1800s to early 1900s show higher concentrations of same-sex households first in Lower Downtown, migrating to Upper Downtown then to North Capitol Hill, demonstrating evidence of early "gayborhoods."

Denver grew from 35,000 in 1880 to nearly 135,000 in 1900. With population growth came efforts to tame and sanitize Denver's rowdy pioneer reputation. By this time, church steeples and a few temple towers dominated the skyline. Along with religious and moral doctrine came the social hygiene movement emphasizing sexual continence and strict self-discipline to solve societal ills caused by rapid urbanization. Predictably, a bohemian subculture developed, populated by assorted misfits who defied social and moral conventions. Among them were people who resisted increasingly restrictive definitions of sexual and/or gender behaviors. By the 1930s, Freudian psychology permeated society, singling out homosexual men and women as pariahs for their "aberrant" sexual desires and behaviors that might be "corrected" with treatment. As society began to classify and stigmatize gay people, they began to segregate themselves, creating safer, more private spaces where they could be themselves.

Opened in 1939, the first documented gay bar was the Snake Pit, located in the basement of a restaurant at Seventeenth Street and Glenarm Place. After World War II, Denver became a major military town, swelling the population with young men eager to experiment sexually among themselves and the civilian population. Some gay bars popular with military personnel were officially placed off-limits to service members. The Court Jester opened in 1961 and was followed by a cluster of now-demolished bars along Broadway near Colfax Avenue. In the 1950s, a Denver chapter of the National Mattachine Society was formed to promote positive views and legal reforms regarding homosexuality. The Mattachine Society's 1959 annual national convention was held in Denver. Believing that sharing their information more broadly would change minds, organizers opened the meeting to the public. It was a courageous decision with disastrous consequences, with local and federal law enforcement attending, taking names, and investigating attendees after the convention—a chilling setback with implications that lasted a decade or more. In the mid-1960s, Denver's newspapers warned of the "homosexual menace," reflecting fears of elected officials who felt duty-bound to protect citizens from urban moral decay. Homosexual acts were still illegal in 48 states, psychiatrists still defined homosexuality as a mental illness, and most religions denounced homosexuality as a grave sin. Denver's LGBTQ community remained deeply closeted until the early 1970s. The nation was still influenced by the ultra-conservative "Lavender Scare" mentality earlier promoted by Sen. Joseph McCarthy and FBI chief J. Edgar Hoover, equating homosexuality with communism and moral rot. Being exposed as queer often meant the loss of one's livelihood, family, reputation, and even home.

The June 1969 Stonewall Uprising in New York City made national headlines, sparking local organizing efforts across the country. Within a year, a gay liberation group formed in Denver. In 1971, Colorado was the third state—the first west of the Mississippi—to decriminalize sodomy, thanks to two Republicans who sponsored the bill. Simultaneously the legislature outlawed "public indecency" to include same-sex public displays of affection, which a court overruled in 1974.

In 1972, the Gay Coalition of Denver (GCD) formed, and on October 23, 1973, it organized a mass peaceful protest at a Denver City Council meeting against repressive city laws and discriminatory enforcement. Just weeks later, Denver City Council repealed four ordinances used against LGBTQ people. Known today as "Denver's Stonewall," the City of Denver officially commemorated the 50th anniversary of the event on October 23, 2023. GCD's victory laid the foundation for future activism to strengthen the LGBTQ community. Since the late 1980s, advances in LGBTQ rights have progressed steadily with Denver City Council's adoption of Denver's inclusive human rights ordinance in 1990, statewide hate crimes legislation enacted in 2001, employment nondiscrimination and two-parent adoption signed into law in 2007, civil unions recognized in 2013, and same-sex marriage recognition in 2014 by a US district court decision.

LGBTQ Denver chronicles more than half a century of the city's progress toward social, political, and economic equality for lesbians, gays, bisexuals, transgender people, and others who identify with the movement for sexual and gender freedom. In some ways, Denver's progress parallels that of other mid-size American cities, and in other ways, Denver has been ahead of the curve, including some notable "firsts" highlighted here in this book. Because Colorado laws and policies affect Denver, the state's more conservative rural and suburban areas have at times impeded social progress. While important, public policy is but one measure of the LGBTQ community's growth. *LGBTQ Denver* attempts to inclusively portray how our diverse community came to thrive socially, culturally, spiritually, and—important in Colorado—recreationally.

The book is organized in approximate (and overlapping) chronological order focusing on events or periods that prompted new surges of LGBTQ engagement and activism. For example, in 1977, volunteers began showing up in droves, moved to action by Anita Bryant's highly visible Save Our Children campaign to repeal gay rights in Miami. The former Miss Oklahoma became an easy target for anger over the campaign's dehumanizing characterization of gay people. In the 1980s, community mobilization to support people with AIDS attracted hundreds of volunteers and donors. In the early 1990s, Colorado's Amendment 2, a ballot initiative to constitutionally eradicate LGBTQ rights, attracted thousands of human rights supporters, gay and straight, to campaign against it, then after it passed, to overturn it at the US Supreme Court. The violent murder of Matthew Shepard in 1998 mobilized a younger generation of activists to push for hate crimes legislation and create antiviolence programs. As conservatives pushed to outlaw same-sex marriage, a long push began to create partnership registries, recognize domestic partnerships, authorize civil unions, and finally, issue marriage licenses to same-sex couples. Along the way, LGBTQ individuals began running for office, winning, and passing pro-LGBTQ legislation.

Despite the best of intentions, this book leaves out more than it can include. The most significant challenge facing those documenting LGBTQ history is the simple fact that, until recent years, so little evidence exists for public use, especially photographs. In addition to the collection of the author's own photographs, *LGBTQ Denver* includes images generously contributed from several institutional collections as noted in the acknowledgments. Likewise, several individuals have generously offered images from their collections. May future historians of Denver's LGBTQ community have access to more evidence from a wider range of sources.

LGBTQ Denver is offered in a spirit of optimism—a hope that readers will see how courage, perseverance, and a strong sense of justice can change our world for the better and change ourselves in the process. While a few of us can write our history, it takes all of us to write our future. May our history provide inspiration for the journey ahead.

One

BEFORE 1970

Denver was founded on November 22, 1858, on land granted by treaty to the Arapaho people seven years earlier. By 1861, white man's laws were instituted to civilize the stolen territory, including a law against "the infamous crime against nature"—sodomy. A century would pass before the September 1959 national convention of the Mattachine Society introduced the prospering Queen City of the Plains to a radical idea: same-sex love should be decriminalized, depathologized, and destigmatized, and that homophiles (Greek for "lover of same") should not suffer discrimination. Of course, same-sex-loving and gender-variant people inhabited the land where Denver was built all along. Many indigenous North American tribes embraced their sexually and gender-variant members. Today, many of these people consider themselves "Two-Spirited."

Mattachine's homophiles naively believed they were normal people except for what they did in private. Mainstream society begged to differ. Homosexuality was a moral threat. Undercover police and FBI agents attended Mattachine's convention and took names, leading to investigations of and consequences for some attendees. But both male-dominated Mattachine and its lesbian counterpart, the Daughters of Bilitis, got the ball rolling in the 1950s to challenge deeply embedded beliefs that homosexuality was sick, sinful, illegal, and even unpatriotic. No wonder the people today collectively called LGBTQ went to great lengths to hide their personal lives and destroy the evidence, making it hard for historians to reconstruct how they lived and loved.

But fragments have surfaced: accounts of cross-dressed men engaging in prostitution, a cluster of lesbians studying spirituality, train-riding hoboes luring adventurous youth into "abominations," women who lived as men finally outed as they were readied for burial, transient young men cavorting at the YMCA, and court records of men accused of "unspeakable depravity." But other sources paint a brighter picture. In *Gay American History* (1976), historian Jonathan Katz cites an early-20th-century letter from a gay Denver professor to the German sexologist Magnus Hirschfeld describing a surprisingly robust gay male society. "I know quite a number of homosexuals in Denver, personally or by hearsay," he wrote, among them "five musicians, three teachers, three art dealers, one minister, one judge, two actors, one florist, and one women's tailor."

Well into the 1960s, reporters and politicians warned of a mounting homosexual threat. Was Denver becoming a gay haven? They failed to understand that it always had been. As the city started cracking down, pressure built inside Denver's gay closets. Before long, those closet doors would bust wide open.

Two-Spirit People. In describing the customs of indigenous peoples, the earliest white people venturing west reported the existence of biological males, and some females, who adopted the dress and social roles of the opposite gender and were held in high esteem within their communities. One of the most famous was We'wha, a Zuni cultural ambassador and weaver who accompanied a delegation that met Pres. Grover Cleveland in 1886. Among tribes who lived where Denver is today, Arapaho Two-Spirit people were called *hoxuxunó*, Cheyenne were *he'eman*, and Southern Ute were *tuwasawits*. (Photograph by John K. Hillers, courtesy of the National Archives and Records Administration.)

Honoring Indigenous Traditions. Members of the Two-Spirit Society of Denver march in the 2011 Pride parade. According to the 2-Spirited People of the 1st Nations website, "Our Elders tell us of people who were gifted among all beings because they carried two spirits: that of male and female. These individuals were looked upon as a third gender in many cases and in almost all cultures they were honored and revered. Today, Two-Spirited people are Native people who are gay, lesbian, bisexual, transgendered, other-gendered, and third/fourth-gendered individuals that walk carefully between the worlds and between the genders." (Photograph by iagoarchangel.)

ADVENTURE DREW YOUNG MEN WEST. "Go west, young man, and grow up with the country," Horace Greeley famously exhorted a young friend in 1854. In the earliest days of Western migration, single men arrived in droves to advance the vision of "Manifest Destiny"—to civilize all of North America with democracy and capitalism—a much-disputed legacy today. Lacking female companionship, and perhaps preferring male society, some men in these all-male enclaves formed enduring intimate bonds with "pardners" whose stories were buried with them. (Courtesy of Phil Nash.)

PIONEER MEN MOVING WEST. The vast majority of the West's earliest settlers from the east were men. Some sought adventure and fortune, some were escaping the social and moral conformity of established communities back east, and still others were running from their past. While one cannot know the sexual identity of frontiersmen who posed together in photography's early days, many left behind permanent visual records of shared affection. (Courtesy of Phil Nash.)

13

VICTORIAN CROSS-DRESSER. A few early Denver newspaper accounts reported police encounters with men dressed as women, usually around Denver's notorious Market Street brothel district. While rare, cross-dressing was practiced by both sexes, sometimes for entertainment and sometimes to disguise one's gender while fleeing from the law. Some women dressed as men to find work. (Courtesy of Phil Nash.)

8081—Gold Miners and their friends, Colo., U. S. A.

EARLY WEST "BACHELOR MARRIAGES." These anonymous miners appear to share a domestic arrangement in the 19th-century gold diggings west of Denver. In her book *Roaring Camp* about life in the early West, Susan Lee Johnson writes, "Men routinely shared beds in mining communities and on the range, and cowboys and miners settled into partnerships that other men recognized (and sometimes referred to) as 'bachelor marriages.'" (Courtesy of the Library of Congress.)

WALT WHITMAN'S DENVER VISIT.
The great American poet who
published sensual verses about
comradely love visited Denver in
1879 as he toured the American
West. Some scholars believe that
Whitman was America's earliest
advocate for gay liberation, while
some biographers downplay
or ignore the explicitly erotic
language in some of his poems.
In *Specimen Days*, he lavished
praise on the young city, even
wishing he could spend his final
years in Denver. "And the best
was the men," he wrote, "three-
fourths of them large, able, calm,
alert, American." (Photograph
by Matthew Brady, courtesy
of the Library of Congress.)

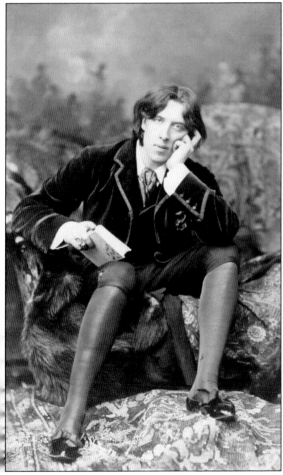

DENVER WELCOMES OSCAR WILDE. In
April 1882, Denver audiences filled
the newly opened Tabor Grand Opera
House to hear the already notorious
28-year-old Irish writer and aesthete
lecture about interior decoration.
According to one reporter's account,
"Mr. Wilde is in appearance not so
effeminate as some people would have
the public believe. He is tall, with broad
shoulders, and moves with the strong,
steady step of a coal-heaver." Wilde was
later imprisoned in strait-laced Britain
for pushing the boundaries of same-sex
love. (Photograph by Napoleon Sarony.)

THE WINDSOR DISTRICT. The area today known as Lower Downtown was early Denver's thriving business center, complete with a red-light district that included cross-dressed male entertainers and sex workers. Historian Edward Scott pinpoints early gay life in and around the Windsor Hotel (opened in 1880, demolished in 1960): "The one block stretch between the Windsor and St. Charles Hotels housed one of Denver's early bohemian communities during the final years of the 19th century, and the Windsor Turkish Baths—at the lower end of the district at 18th and Larimer—was catering to middle and upper-class homosexual white men by the 1890s." (Courtesy of the Library of Congress.)

A VICTORIAN CROSS-DRESSER. This anonymous man dressed in elegant female attire was not out of the ordinary in the late 19th century. Male entertainers performing as women were seen in Denver as early as June 1876 according to historian Edward Scott, who recounts the appearance of the "the great original and only Alf Wyman" at a downtown theater. "Though he was the first female impersonator recorded to have performed on a Denver stage, he was likely preceded by many," writes Scott. Female illusionists were a fairly standard feature on the vaudeville circuit, often as headliners, until the end of World War I. (Courtesy of Phil Nash.)

CASUAL COWBOY INTIMACY. These real-life cowboys from the late 19th century apparently have not gotten the memo from Hollywood about the masculine code of the West defining men as rough and tough and supremely heterosexual. These fellows seem to enjoy lounging intimately with each other on a break from riding the range. In *Queer Cowboys*, author Chris Packard writes, "Emotional bonds, social bonds, and physical bonds characterize these same-sex friendships, not to mention a great deal of unguarded affection and, I argue, erotic attraction." (Courtesy of Deak Wooten.)

THE LAST BIG DIVIDE. Tender relationships between men in the early West were neither stigmatized nor scorned, as evidenced by this 1897 photograph of a frontier man mourning the death of his partner. In his poem "The Lost Pardner," cowboy poet Badger Clark commemorates such a friendship that ended when one man died: "We loved each other in the way men do, and never spoke about it, Al and me. But we both knowed, and knowin' it so true was more than any woman's kiss could be." For the complete poem, visit allpoetry.com/the-lost-pardner. (Courtesy of the Library of Congress.)

17

"Boston Marriage" Frees Women. These unidentified women from a late-19th-century postcard pose in a staged domestic situation suggesting they may be a female couple. Boston marriages, taken from Henry James's 1880s novel *The Bostonians*, refers to women of independent financial means bonding with other women for intimate and possibly sexual companionship in order to remain free of marital obligations. While lesbian history is especially challenging to trace, Denver gay historians have found evidence of dual-female households in early 20th-century census records. (Courtesy of Phil Nash.)

It's Fun to Stay at the YMCA. Built in 1906, Downtown Denver's YMCA long served as a magnet for gay, bi, and questioning men, especially new arrivals in earlier times when it offered cheap dormitory accommodations. In the 1960s, responding to media and political warnings of Denver becoming a "homosexual haven," the "Y" clamped down, though not fully quashing its reputation as a cruising zone. In the 1970s and 1980s, as gay life offered safer alternatives, the Y's reputation as a gay connecting point diminished. (Courtesy of the Library of Congress.)

HISTORIC SHIP TAVERN. This nautically decorated pub in Downtown Denver's historic Brown Palace Hotel was never a gay bar, per se. But before bars catering to an exclusively gay clientele were commonplace, it was known among circles of quietly gay men as a friendly watering hole where one could meet other like-minded gentlemen. (Photograph by Phil Nash.)

DOWNTOWN DENVER GAY BEACON. Most early gay bars were hard to find, often with alley entrances so patrons could come and go unnoticed—but not the Court Jester, sometimes referred to as "the CJ." Established in 1963 at 1617 Court Place, the CJ's gaudy neon sign lit up the night. According to historian Tom Noel's 1973 notes for his master's thesis on the history of Denver's bars, gay guidebooks rated the CJ as "PE" for "piss-elegant." A hot spot in the early 1970s serving hundreds of patrons on weekend nights, the CJ's popularity waned as newer bars opened, finally being demolished in 1981. (Courtesy of the Denver Public Library.)

DENVER HOSTS MATTACHINE SOCIETY CONVENTION, 1959. The Albany Hotel in downtown Denver hosted the sixth national convention of the Mattachine Society in September 1959. Organizers allowed nonmembers from the public to attend, hoping to broaden awareness of Mattachine's mission. Law enforcement officers took advantage of the invitation to collect the names of attendees. In its newsletter (opposite page) after hosting the convention, the Denver Area Council credits itself for news coverage representing "progress in bringing to public attention information about a subject that has for too long caused tragedy because of prejudice and ignorance." (Left, courtesy of the Denver Public Library; opposite, courtesy of Phil Nash.)

MATTACHINE PIONEERS LEAD THE PARADE. Forty years after the 1959 Mattachine Society national convention in Denver, four surviving members of the Denver chapter served as grand marshals of the 1999 Pride parade. Pictured from left to right are Earl Gebhardt, William Reynard, Roland Karcher, and Elver Barker. Barker, using the pseudonym Carl Harding, was the lead organizer of Denver Mattachine beginning in 1956 and a prolific writer for the cause. (Photograph by Phil Nash.)

| For Further Information About Mattachine—WRITE: | National Headquarters: **Mattachine Society, Inc.** 693 Mission Street San Francisco 5 EXbrook 7-0773 | —OR your nearest Area Council: DENVER OFFICE P. O. BOX 7035 CAPITOL HILL STATION DENVER 6, COLORADO |

BREAK-THROUGH
in the Conspiracy of SILENCE

Long a barrier to the dissemination of accurate facts about varied human sexual behavior--and especially about homosexual behavior--is the widespread "taboo" shown by the press and other mass communications media.

Homosexuality, unless described as a vice--or acts of degeneracy—is not an acceptable subject, most editors say. In 1958 in New York, Mattachine public relations representatives attempted to get an announcement of the Society's annual meeting in that city published in newspapers. The effort failed. In one newspaper at least, an item reached the top city editor before it was vetoed for print.

During the year, however, some cracks in the 'conspiracy of silence' were noted in the general press. A magazine in the "men's group" published a letter setting forth accurately Mattachine aims and principles as a follow-up to an erroneous reference to the Society in a previous article. Another magazine, in the so-called "scandal" group, printed a long and generally accurate article on the Mattachine in June 1959. Articles from the Mattachine Review were reprinted in three nationally circulated publications in Canada and the U. S. during the past year-- all with credit to the source.

But it remained for the publicity efforts made largely by the Denver Area Council in advance of the recent 6th Annual Convention in that city to get the Society's first significant publicity in two daily newspapers--Denver Post and Rocky Mountain News. Advance stories told who was going to speak, where the convention was to be held, and mentioned it was open to the public. An interview with national officers appeared in each paper. Reporters covered the important sessions. Final items listed the officers elected. Reprinted inside this folder are clippings from these newspapers.

Following the convention, Denver officers of the Society wrote thanks to these newspapers for the splendid coverage. This resulted in a final round of Mattachine publicity--presented in the inevitable format of "pro" and "con". The four letters published appear on the back page of this folder.

Mattachine is proud to report these "breakthroughs in the conspiracy of silence." The reports herein represent progress in bringing to public attention information about a subject that has for too long caused tragedy because of prejudice and ignorance. The articles reprinted inside were read by more than a half million persons.

OLDEST GAY BAR STILL STANDING. The R&R Lounge, at 4958 East Colfax Avenue, has been in business since the 1950s, first as a "mixed" bar called the Coral Lounge and renamed in the 1970s for former owners Rick and Roger, according to a 2017 *Westword* article. The R&R is off the beaten path, "just a chill neighborhood bar that's also a gay bar," wrote *Westword* contributor Sarah McGill. (Photograph by Phil Nash.)

REVVING THE ENGINES OF PRIDE. The Rocky Mountaineers Motorcycle Club (RMMC) was established on November 18, 1968, by founding members Bob Connell ("Top Hand," or president; first row, second from left), Jim Kane, John Fenner, Duke St. Pierre, Frank St. Cyr, Bob Lundgren (first row, far right), George Edwards, Allen Dyer, Hal Haney, and Wally Bruce (second row, far left). None of the RMMC members pictured in this summer 1969 photograph are known to be living. In RMMC's early years, only members' first names and last initials were used in written materials. (Courtesy of Bill Olson.)

Two

Stonewall Ripples Reach Denver

The Stonewall riots that erupted in New York's Greenwich Village on June 28, 1969, were "the shot heard round the world," writes historian Lillian Faderman. Stonewall triggered a tsunami of activism as news about LGBTQ people defying police oppression traveled across the globe. Pride celebrations around the world commemorate Stonewall.

Eighteen hundred miles away, Stonewall's ripples crested in Denver on October 23, 1973, as several hundred LGBTQ folks jammed Denver City Council chambers demanding an end to police harassment. "Denver's Stonewall" was organized by the Gay Coalition of Denver (GCD), founded a year earlier in the Congress Park apartment of Gerald Gerash and Lynn Tamlin along with cofounders Terry Mangan, Jane Dundee, and Mary Sassatelli. GCD grew quickly with political and legal committees, a speaker's bureau, a library, a hotline, "coming out" classes, and discussion groups.

GCD's protest was in response to Denver's vice squad ramping up arrests of gay men on trumped-up sexual solicitation charges, a misdemeanor that could cause arrestees to lose jobs and homes, as well as face public disgrace. Earlier in 1973, GCD had sued to end the illegal arrests and halt discriminatory police harassment, such as issuing jaywalking tickets near gay bars and arresting people for same-sex kissing in public.

Led by attorney Gerash, GCD prepared charts, graphs, and testimony. Forced by a hostile council president to wait three hours to speak, GCD's 35 registered speakers were granted only 30 minutes to make their case. Some council members objected, so the time allotted was extended. GCD's "teach-in," as Gerash described it, lasted late into the night. "Slowly, they became willing to listen, and, at the end, some even complimented the protesters," said Gerash. Within weeks, the city council repealed four laws that led to the protest. A year later, GCD scored another victory by winning its lawsuit, requiring police to stop arresting people for same-sex kissing in public and to stop "oppressive and harsh police activity against homosexually oriented persons or establishments where they gather." It was a first for the nation, "burnishing Denver's reputation as a leading center for gay rights," said Gerash. For more information, search "Denver's Gay Revolt" on YouTube.

Impressed by GCD's presentation, a gay bathhouse owner handed Gerash $2,000 in cash. With the unexpected donation, GCD opened an office and hired a coordinator. The office remained open for about a year before closing due to a lack of funds in 1975.

DENVER GAY LIBERATION, JANUARY 1971. The Stonewall uprising led to the short-lived Gay Liberation Front in New York and inspired copycat organizations nationwide. In Robert C. Steele's book *Banned In California*, a biography of activist Jim Foshee, he includes Foshee's observations about Denver Gay Liberation. The group held a coffeehouse and meetings to discuss gay strategies, including a gathering space for the community. In November 1971, over 200 gays participated in a protest against the Vietnam War under the Gay Liberation Front banner, the first time anyone marched under a gay banner in Denver. The group disbanded after about 18 months. (Courtesy of History Colorado.)

HUNDREDS CROWD INTO COUNCIL CHAMBERS. On October 23, 1973, several hundred lesbians, gay men, and allies jammed into Denver City Council Chambers to urge changes to city ordinances that singled out LGBTQ people for discriminatory enforcement by Denver police. Organized by the Gay Coalition of Denver, many attendees wore green carnations, a symbol created by Oscar Wilde in the 1890s to announce one's queerness publicly. The hearing lasted into the wee hours of the morning. In the front middle of the photograph are, from left to right, GCD leaders Terry Mangan, Cordell Boyce, and Gerald Gerash. (Courtesy of Gerald Gerash.)

COUNCILMAN IS NOT AMUSED. Denver City councilman L. Don Wyman's expression captures the sense of bewilderment that many of his colleagues felt at the barrage of testimony offered by GCD speakers. Testimony began late in the evening and continued for more than three hours before the last speakers were finished. (Courtesy of Gerald Gerash.)

ATTORNEY ATTACKS "LEWDNESS" LAW. Gay Coalition of Denver cofounder Gerald Gerash, an attorney and human rights activist, cites proof of a law's discriminatory purpose. "It says private conversations . . . in particular those that have sexual connotations are illegal. Secondly, I wish to make the point that the only force in this city that wants to make these private conversations illegal is the vice bureau of the Denver Police Department." (Courtesy of Gerald Gerash.)

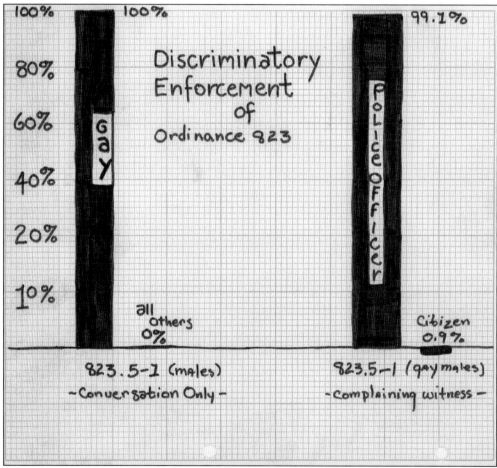

THE "OBSCENE" DATA SLIDE. Volunteer attorneys for the Gay Coalition of Denver spent months reviewing arrest records of people charged under Denver's lewdness ordinance. They found that 100 percent of the arrestees were gay men and that more than 99 percent of the complaints were made by Denver vice officers, not the public. When asking permission to display the data, Gerald Gerash referred to the information as "obscene," momentarily causing council president Robert Koch to refuse the request. Gerash clarified that what was "obscene" was the extent of discriminatory enforcement. (Courtesy of History Colorado.)

SPEAKERS WAIT THEIR TURN. Among the 36 speakers at the October 23, 1973, Denver City Council meeting were, from left to right, Rick Griffin, Liz Matthews, and Marge Johnson. In her remarks, Johnson starkly highlighted the unequal treatment of gay people under the law: "I cannot hold hands with another woman in public. I cannot walk in public with my arm around another woman. I cannot kiss another woman in public. Yet these expressions of affection between a man and a woman are acceptable since what they do is seen as courting behavior, and what I do as lewd and lascivious." (Courtesy of Gerald Gerash.)

AMERICAN CIVIL LIBERTIES UNION ICON. Denver attorney William F. "Bill" Reynard (1918–2008) was a civil liberties activist who was a longtime leader in the Colorado Chapter of the American Civil Liberties Union and a member of the Denver Mattachine Society during the 1950s. Reynard testified at the October 23, 1973, Denver City Council hearings. (Courtesy of Gerald Gerash.)

ACCIDENTAL ADVOCATE. On October 23, 1973, recent college graduate Phil Krasnowski Wade planned on an evening at the Door, a downtown gay bar near the Denver City and County Building. He found a locked entrance with a flyer urging would-be patrons to head to nearby city council chambers for the hearing to rescind antigay ordinances. He walked to the meeting and signed up to speak. A few years later, Wade started a social support group for LGBTQ teachers at a time when conservative political efforts focused on expunging gay teachers from schools in some areas of the country. (Courtesy of Gerald Gerash.)

TERRY MANGAN, HISTORIAN AND PIONEER. Terry Mangan's day job in 1973 was with the Colorado Historical Society (today known as History Colorado), where he published *Colorado On Glass*, a critically acclaimed book of early Colorado photographs. In his off hours, Mangan was one of Denver's earliest gay organizers, helping found Denver Gay Liberation in 1971 and in 1972 cofounding the Gay Coalition of Denver, where he established a library of LGBT literature. The Terry Mangan Memorial Library lives on at the Center on Colfax more than a half-century later. (Courtesy of Gerald Gerash.)

FIRST GAY OFFICE. At the conclusion of the Gay Coalition of Denver's presentation to the Denver City Council, a San Francisco gay bath owner handed Gerald Gerash $2,000 in cash to support GCD's work. With this unexpected gift, GCD opened an office at 1450 Pennsylvania Street and hired Cordell Boyce as a full-time coordinator. (Photograph by Phil Nash.)

FIRST GAY COFFEEHOUSE. In the early 1970s, the Gay Coalition of Denver operated the weekly Approaching Lavender Coffee House at 1122 East Seventeenth Avenue offering music, dance, films, and poetry readings—entertainment for those seeking social alternatives to gay bars. The space, then home to Denver Free University, is now a unique home decor and toy store. (Photograph by Phil Nash.)

EARLY MEDIA PROTEST. Phil Allen (left) and Jim Foshee picket Channel 9, then Denver's ABC network affiliate, on October 8, 1974, when the local station broadcasted an episode of the popular television program *Marcus Welby, M.D.* entitled "The Outrage." The drama was about a male pedophile attacking a teenage male, inaccurately connecting pedophilia with homosexuality. The National Gay Task Force organized a nationwide protest urging local stations to not air the offending episode and to boycott the program's sponsors. While the episode was dropped in many markets, it aired in Denver. (Courtesy of Gerald Gerash.)

COUNCILMAN REMEMBERS GAY REVOLT. At a 30th-anniversary commemoration of the Denver Gay Revolt in October 2003, former city councilman Irving Hook speaks on the steps of the City and County Building as council president Elba Wedgeworth looks on. On the night of the "gay revolt," Hook defended the right of Gay Coalition of Denver representatives to bring their grievances to the city council while some of his colleagues threatened to cut the speakers off. According to GCD organizer Gerald Gerash, Hook was sympathetic to the GCD because, as a Jew, he understood the importance of protesting discrimination. (Photograph by Phil Nash.)

Three

A COMMUNITY
TAKES SHAPE

Boosted by the Gay Coalition of Denver's victories and the brief but successful experience of a staffed headquarters, Gerash and others began laying the groundwork for a permanent community center offering programs, services, and community meeting space. After GCD's success in getting Denver's anti-drag law repealed, the newly created Imperial Court of the Rocky Mountain Empire (ICRME) and the Tobie Foundation, both affiliated with the drag entertainment and gay bar culture, began organizing gay pride events alongside GCD. On Saturday, June 29, 1974, Denver's first Gay-In was held at Cheesman Park with a few dozen people attending. GCD's newsletter reported the attendees all received balloons imprinted with "Gay Pride." On Sunday, June 29, 1975, the second Gay-In at Cheesman drew an estimated 500 people, according to the *Scene*, a gay publication owned by Ron Wilson, one of the event's coordinators. The report said net proceeds from the event would benefit a future gay community service center.

Two months earlier, cooperation among the more politically oriented GCD, the more socially focused bar and drag communities, and several gay religious groups led to the formation of Unity, a coalition of gay organizations. About 15–20 people attended Unity's first meeting in April 1975. Bill Olson, representative of the Rocky Mountaineers Motorcycle Club, recalls that the earliest Unity members were the GCD, ICRME, RMMC, Tobie Foundation, Lesbian Task Force of NOW, Boulder Gay Liberation Front, Metropolitan Community Church of the Rockies, and Dignity/Denver.

Gerash proposed that Unity serve as a forum to share information and promote understanding while working to establish a gay community center. The vote in favor was unanimous. Soon a savings account was established with deposits of $380 from the 1975 Gay-In and $35 from ICRME Emperor II Bucky Reed's "Something Different" event. As news of a future gay community center spread, Unity's membership swelled to more than 30 organizations and businesses.

On September 18–19, 1976, Unity held a retreat at the Bunkhouse guest lodge in Breckenridge to lay plans, leading to the incorporation of the Gay Community Center of Colorado (GCCC) on November 19, 1976. Over the winter and spring, committees met, fundraisers were held, and a hiring process was conducted. Phil Nash was selected as the center's coordinator. On August 1, 1977, the GCCC rented space at 1436 Lafayette Street from the First Unitarian Society of Denver and officially opened on August 21 with a ribbon-cutting and open house for about 100 attendees.

First Legal Gay Marriage. In April 1975, Boulder County clerk Clela Rorex issued marriage licenses to six same-sex couples, seeing nothing in state law requiring applicants to be of the opposite sex. Richard Adams and Anthony Sullivan were united at a ceremony at the First Unitarian Church of Denver witnessed by Metropolitan Community Church of the Rockies pastor Charlie Arehart. The couple remained together until Adams died in 2012. Sullivan, an Australian citizen, was denied immigrant status by the United States but finally obtained a green card in 2016. *Limited Partnership* is a documentary about their relationship. (Courtesy of History Colorado.)

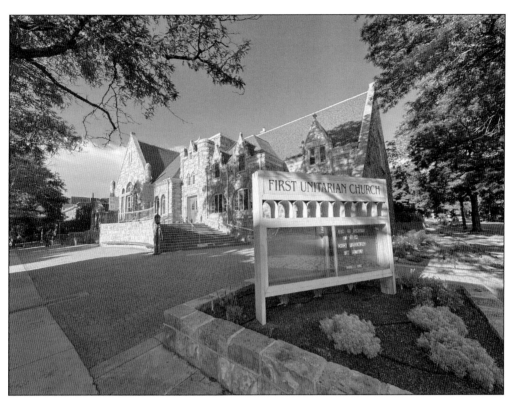

FIRST UNITARIAN CHURCH. With its congregation's mission enmeshed with social justice advocacy, the 1890s-era landmark at 1400 Lafayette Street has hosted many LGBTQ firsts dating from the 1950s, when it provided space to the Denver Mattachine Society. In 1974, it became the first long-term home for Metropolitan Community Church of the Rockies; in 1975, the site of the first same-sex wedding in Colorado; in 1977, the first landlord of the Gay Community Center of Colorado; and in the 1990s, the site of early organizing meetings against Amendment 2. (Photograph by Phil Nash.)

PASTOR CHARLIE AREHART. Rev. Charlie Arehart was elected to serve as the first pastor of the fledgling Metropolitan Community Church of the Rockies (MCCR) in November 1973. He served as pastor for nearly 22 years before leaving for other opportunities outside Denver in 1995. Arehart was widely known and respected for his leadership and involvement with many organizations including the Colorado AIDS Project, the Alexander Foundation, the Gay and Lesbian Community Center, Parents and Friends of Lesbians and Gays, and more. He is pictured here at a Pride parade in the early 1980s. (Photograph by Phil Nash.)

PRIDE COMES TO DENVER. This flyer advertises Denver's second Pride celebration in June 1975 sponsored by the *Scene* (an early gay newspaper), the Gay Coalition of Denver, Dignity (gay Catholics), Gay Students Association (Metro State), Boulder Gay Liberation Front, the Tobie Foundation, and the Imperial Court of the Rocky Mountain Empire. The *Scene* reported an estimated 500 attendees who consumed 11 kegs during the afternoon beer bust. The "Gay Olympics" consisted of a tug-of-war held in the fountain in front of the Cheesman Pavilion. (Courtesy of Bill Olson.)

FIRST PRIDE PARADE, 1976. After two years of "Gay-In" Pride celebrations in Cheesman Park, in 1976, Christopher Sloan of the Tobie Foundation secured a permit and the group organized a parade that started in Cheesman, proceeded west on East Colfax Avenue, and ended in Civic Center Park at the Greek Theater. In this photograph, Scotti Carlyle (center), Empress II of the Imperial Court, holds the historical parade permit as the parade lines up. Holding the banner are Gary Edwards (left) and Paul Brown, with John Sheppard on the far right. Immediately behind the banner, from left to right, are Michael Nolan, Michael Procopio, and Craig Ball. (Courtesy of Bill Olson.)

LESBIAN BIKERS AT FIRST PRIDE PARADE. Free Spirit Motorcycle Club was a lesbian motorcycle club that existed from 1976 to 1979. These riders began a long tradition of prominently featuring women motorcyclists in annual Pride parades, colloquially known as "dykes on bikes." Pictured from left to right are Lee "Twiggy" Stiffins, Cathie ?, Pam "Miski" Miskimins, and an unidentified passenger. (Courtesy of Bill Olson.)

OUT FRONT PREMIER ISSUE. "There's no turning back," announces *Out Front* on the masthead of its inaugural issue. The paper includes articles about stepped-up police harassment around gay bars, high rates of VD (for venereal disease, now called sexually transmitted infections) among gays, an article about gay hustling, a fashion column from the gay-owned Haberdashery clothing store, a negative film review of *The Dutchess and the Dirtwater Fox* (filmed in Central City), and lots of news and ads about the Imperial Court's third Coronation ball. The back page carried the iconic Triangle Lounge ad featuring a denim-covered man's crotch. (Courtesy of History Colorado.)

PHIL PRICE LAUNCHES OUT FRONT. A recent graduate of the University of Colorado at Boulder, fledgling publisher Phil Price launched *Out Front* on April 2, 1976, promising "to bring Colorado a long-awaited, much-needed quality journal for the gay community." Price is pictured here in the early 1980s. Originally published monthly, *Out Front* soon began publishing biweekly. Price died of AIDS in 1993, with Greg Montoya and Jay Klein taking the helm until 2012, when they sold it to Jerry Cunningham. In 2020, Maggie Phillips and Addison Herron-Wheeler became majority owners and copublishers. (Photograph by Phil Nash.)

CRUISING CENTRAL. During the 1970s, the grounds of the Colorado State Capitol and its circular drive were the favored spot for male hustlers and their motorized clients, the subject of a feature story in *Out Front's* inaugural issue. At twilight, "Sodomy Circle" came alive after the legislature recessed. In 1979, the issue came to a head, with the press quoting one legislator denouncing the "fruities" and another rural lawmaker offering to solve the problem by mounting the capitol dome with his rifle. (Photograph by Phil Nash.)

BIG MAMA RAG, 1972–1984. *Big Mama Rag* (*BMR*) was a Denver-based feminist newspaper initially organized by a collective of 13 women. The first issue appeared in 1973, and by a year later, circulation had reached 3,000. *BMR* reflected the socialist-feminist perspectives of the all-volunteer collective and covered the women's movement and a broad range of social justice issues including lesbian oppression. (Courtesy of History Colorado.)

BIG MAMA RAG ROAD TRIP. In 1976, the staff of *Big Mama Rag* drove to Nebraska to attend a Women In Print conference. Pictured from left to right are Eileen Bresnahan, Kate Sharp, Tea Schook, Vicki Piotter, Peg Rapp, and Clair Strawn. Piotter and Rapp were also founders of the Woman to Woman Feminist Book Center. (Courtesy of History Colorado.)

WOMAN TO WOMAN. This stained-glass window depicting two women facing each other hung in the storefront of Woman to Woman Feminist Book Center, which opened at 2023 East Colfax Avenue on August 15, 1975, and closed in 1983. Founders Vicky Piotter, Peg Rapp, and Kay Young operated it a collective organization that offered books for sale, a lending library, classes, poetry readings, and more. Its switchboard fielded thousands of calls from women seeking help with an array of legal, medical, and human services needs. The storefront provided a meeting space, making it a center for women's organizing and networking. (Courtesy of History Colorado.)

ROCKY MOUNTAIN GAY RADIO. In July 1977, *Colorado Gaybreak*, the first radio program by and for the LGBTQ community in the Rocky Mountain region, began airing on KWBZ-AM radio, with a broadcasting range from Cheyenne, Wyoming, to Pueblo, Colorado. Bob Steele (right), an experienced producer, oversaw a volunteer staff who kept the weekly one-hour talk-radio show on the air until March 1978, when a new station owner canceled its contract. Ken Watts (left) was the show's comoderator working alongside female moderator Jan Grimm and volunteers Jim Foshee, Roar Poliac, Jan Hoegh, and Will Guthrie. (Courtesy of Robert C. Steele.)

Bunkhouse Retreat Charts Center's Future. In September 1976, Unity held a two-day retreat to plan the future Gay Community Center of Colorado at the Bunkhouse Lodge, a gay resort in Breckenridge. Then owned by Rudy Gardner, the Bunkhouse grew from a 19th-century log cabin to a comfortable guest lodge that began welcoming a gay clientele in 1972. The planning meeting resulted in the new organization's name, a blueprint for governance, and a work plan for incorporation as a Colorado nonprofit organization on November 19, 1976. (Courtesy of Phil Nash.)

Gay Community Center Opens. On August 21, 1977, the Gay Community Center of Colorado opened its doors at 1436 Lafayette Street in space rented from the nearby First Unitarian Church. Phil Nash, the center's first director, welcomes guests on the front porch of the office. Approximately 100 people attended the opening. For the first several years, the center operated primarily with volunteers with just one paid staff person. Nash led the organization until early 1980, when he became editor of *Out Front*. He was succeeded by Carol Lease. (Courtesy of Phil Nash.)

LOGO T-SHIRTS FOR SALE. Dr. Bob Janowski, one of the volunteer organizers, sells t-shirts with the center's first logo at the August 1977 grand opening event. Janowski was Denver's first known openly gay physician; he built a medical practice caring for hundreds of LGBTQ patients and also wrote "Medical Bag," a health advice column for *Out Front*. (Courtesy of Phil Nash.)

THE CENTER'S FOUNDERS REUNITED. In June 2016, to commemorate the 40th anniversary of the founding of the Gay Community Center of Colorado (today known as the Center on Colfax), seven of the eight living founders reunited for a presentation and panel discussion about the organization's origins. Pictured from left to right are (first row) Gerald Gerash and Phil Nash; (second row) Bill Olson, Bob Janowski, Christopher Sloan, Donaciano Martinez, and Richard Reed. Frank Aguilar was unable to attend. By 2016, more than a dozen of the center's founders had died. (Courtesy of Phil Nash.)

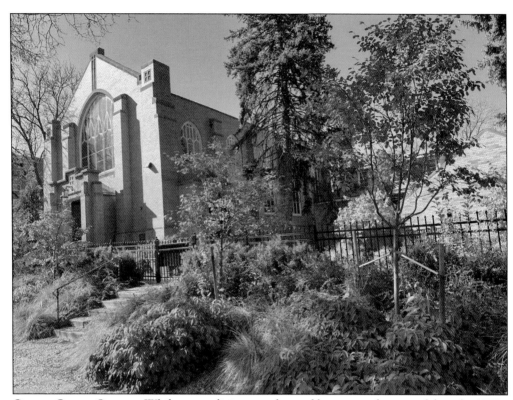

Coming Out at Church. While most religions condemned homosexuality as sinful, in the 1970s, several central Denver churches opened their doors to gay and lesbian groups to meet and begin building community. Beginning in 1978, Warren United Methodist Church, at East Fourteenth Avenue and Gilpin Street, was the meeting place for the weekly Men's Coming Out Group, first organized in 1977 and lasting until the early 2000s. According to founder Don McMaster, weekly attendance often reached 100 people and likely welcomed more than 20,000 men to the facilitated group discussions over the years. No longer a church, Warren Residences provides low-income housing. (Photograph by Phil Nash.)

The Anita Bryant Boomerang Effect. Coming out as gay took on greater urgency in 1977. Former Miss America runner-up Anita Bryant became the spokeswoman for Save Our Children, a Florida-based fundamentalist Christian movement to repeal a gay rights ordinance in Miami. The campaign assumed national dimensions as LGBTQ people everywhere viewed the wholesome Bryant as the face of a political enemy out to destroy hard-won rights and deny equal treatment. Bryant's crusade backfired by drawing newcomers to the growing lesbian/gay movement, including in Denver, swelling attendance at gay pride events and participation in community organizations. (Photograph by Phil Nash.)

BETTY FAIRCHILD, PFLAG PIONEER. The mother of a gay son, Betty Fairchild first joined Parents and Friends of Lesbians and Gays (PFLAG) in Washington, DC. After moving to Denver in the mid-1970s, she formed a similar parent-support group. In 1979, Fairchild published *Now That You Know—A Parent's Guide to Understanding Their Gay and Lesbian Children*, one of the earliest books addressing parents' concerns and helping families through the coming out process. In 1980, PFLAG Denver expanded rapidly after several individuals who attended the 1979 National March on Washington for Lesbian and Gay Rights bought full-page ads in local newspapers advertising the organization's meetings. (Courtesy of Phil Nash.)

PFLAG DENVER LEADER NANCY KEENE. Nance Keene became president of PFLAG Denver in 1980 and enthusiastically led the organization for a dozen years. Keene, pictured at center with gay son Mark (left) and lesbian daughter Meredith, was an energetic and ubiquitous cheerleader for Denver's LGBTQ community. In 1985, she and two others formed PFLAG Denver's AIDS Family Support Group, one of the first of its kind, which eventually helped 700 families cope with the illness and loss of a gay family member. Keene died in 2018. (Courtesy of History Colorado.)

GENDER IDENTITY CENTER. With roots dating back to 1966, the Gender Identity Center (GIC) was formed in 1978 as the result of a study group meeting at the Gay Community Center of Colorado to help people with gender identity issues. It incorporated as a nonprofit organization in 1980. Services included discussion groups for young men, spouses/significant others, new women, male-to-female transitions, and teens as well as workshops on fashion, makeup, voice, and speakers who discussed gender affirmation surgery, hormones, and gender identity. In 2018, GIC was reorganized as the Transgender Center of the Rockies, a program of Mile High Behavioral Health. (Photograph by iagoarchangel.)

PROTESTING POLICE KILLINGS OF TRANS PEOPLE. On July 14, 1977, trans sex worker Eugene Levi was killed during a botched arrest when Denver police officer Daniel O'Hayre's pistol discharged as he attempted to hit Levi. On March 30, 1978, trans sex worker Tony "Irene" DeSoto was shot to death by officer Larry Subia during a plain-clothes arrest for prostitution. Investigations cleared both officers but raised troubling questions. After the second police killing in nine months, the ad hoc Transsexual, Lesbian & Gay Defense mounted a downtown protest march attracting more than 200 people demanding more accountability from police. (Anonymous photographer.)

Four

BUILD IT AND THEY WILL COME

During the 1970s, thousands of LGBTQ people came together to build a strong, vibrant, and welcoming community—one that did not previously exist in Denver outside a few narrow nooks and concealed crannies. Several keystone organizations paved the way for an eruption of LGBTQ social, cultural, and entrepreneurial activities in the 1980s. Some endure, like the Center on Colfax, Metropolitan Community Church of the Rockies, the Imperial Court of the Rocky Mountain Empire, the Denver Gay Men's Chorus, the Denver Women's Chorus, the Mile High Freedom Bands, the Colorado Gay Rodeo Association, Parents and Friends of Lesbians and Gays, the Rocky Mountain Rainbeaus square-dancing club, and many more. Others, like the Leaping Lesbian Follies and Rainbow Society for the Deaf, do not. Some short-lived groups, like the Fleet-Footed Fairies of the Front Range, a running group, and the Women's Outdoors Club were precursors to more permanent sports and recreation organizations. Today, many LGBTQ athletic and recreation groups thrive under the organizational umbrella of Team Colorado USA, which promotes local participation in the worldwide Gay Games. The Professional Social Network of the early 1980s was an early precursor of the Colorado Business Council, later renamed the Colorado LGBTQ Chamber of Commerce. In the early 1980s, the Alexander Foundation, named for the man-loving conqueror Alexander the Great, began holding fundraising cocktail parties in elegant venues then distributing charitable dollars to needy LGBTQ community members and awarding scholarships to LGBTQ students.

Some gay bars also got into the community-building mode recognizing that patrons were looking for more than drinking, dancing, drag, and dates. In the 1980s, the AIDS crisis took an economic toll on bars; gay men were staying home to avoid disease transmission. To bring patrons back, bar owners got creative. BJ's Carousel sponsored art competitions for several years. The Fox Hole built a volleyball "beach." Tracks cohosted many events with LGBTQ nonprofits and advocacy groups. Trivia nights, talent nights, drag-queen bingo, spaghetti dinners, fashion shows, and other themed activities gave patrons more reasons to go out.

Within a decade of Stonewall, Denver's LGBTQ community had grown into a thriving small town within a large city. No longer a hidden gay subculture, by the early 1980s, many doors opened into a thriving, evolving, multidimensional community. Gay men of all backgrounds could join a musical group, a sports team, and a political group. Lesbians could work within the greater feminist movement, join a lesbian motorcycle club, and help mount a women's music festival. Individuals who felt they could not be themselves in their assigned gender began to have resources to help them explore and accomplish a gender transition. Volunteer leaders with ideas and energy kept opening new doors.

THE FUTURE LGBTQ CENTER, 1981. These marchers in the 1981 Pride parade pass in front of the Metropolitan Industrial Bank on East Colfax Avenue en route from Cheesman Park to Civic Center Park. Nearly three decades later, the long-vacant building was purchased and remodeled as the headquarters for the Center on Colfax, which opened in September 2010. After renting space for nearly 35 years, it was the first building the center owned, thanks to a $3-million capital campaign. (Photograph by Phil Nash.)

CAROL LEASE LEADS COMMUNITY CENTER. In 1980, Carol Lease (third row, far left) became the executive director of the newly renamed Gay and Lesbian Community Center of Colorado, helping to attract more lesbian participation in the organization. In this photograph taken at the center's headquarters at 1436 Lafayette Street, Lease is pictured with some board members and volunteers. People in the first row are unidentified. From left to right are (second row) Gwen Hankins, Martha Brummett, Deb Berkowitz, and Orie Thompson; (third row) Lease, Karen Peterson, unidentified woman, Vern Langhofer, and Janet Lewallen; (fourth row) David Holbrook. (Photograph by Phil Nash.)

MATTACHINE COFOUNDER VISITS DENVER. The 1977 documentary *Word Is Out: Stories of Some of Our Lives* featured Mattachine Society cofounder Harry Hay (right), then living with his partner, John Burnside, in northern New Mexico. After Hay and Burnside attended a Denver opening of the film, they visited periodically after making local friends and connections. They introduced some Denver gay men to the radical faery movement then developing in California and later branching into Colorado. Radical faeries emerged in reaction to the rampant stereotyping and commercialization of gay men's lives by seeking closer connections to nature, spirituality, and deeper exploration of gay identity. (Photograph by Phil Nash.)

LGBTQ BUSINESS WELCOME HERE. Since the 1970s, the office building at 1245 East Colfax Avenue at Lafayette Street has rented space to LGBTQ businesses and organizations. Just the first floor has been occupied at various times by the gay-owned Haberdashery clothing store, Out Front Colorado, the Gay and Lesbian Community Center (now the Center on Colfax just across the street), Equality Colorado, and several LGBTQ-owned food and beverage storefronts. (Photograph by Phil Nash.)

COLORADO LESBIANS GAIN VISIBILITY. During the 1970s, the lesbian community developed mostly independent of the gay male community, forming organizations by and for women and starting women-owned businesses. Lesbians-Colorado held two statewide conferences in Denver in September 1979 and November 1980. In 1979, more than 700 women attended 55 workshops and entertainment events. In 1980, more than 1,200 women attended 39 workshops and events. The conferences boosted visibility for the state's lesbian community, created new connections, and launched networks for change. (Photograph by Phil Nash.)

GREAT MEN OF THE ROCKIES. Tim Wilson (second from left) organized Gay Racially and Equal Men Together, a Denver affiliate of the National Association of Black and White Men Together, founded in 1980. GREAT Men created opportunities for interracial gay male couples and single men of both races to socialize. (Photograph by Phil Nash.)

CATEGORY SIX BOOKS. Category Six Books was Denver's first LGBTQ bookstore, named for No. 6 on the Kinsey scale—100 percent homosexual. Located at 909 East Colfax Avenue from 1982 to 1991, the store later moved to 1029 East Eleventh Avenue from 1991 to 1996. The store was founded, owned, and operated by Neil Woodward, left, a library science graduate, pictured here with his partner (and later husband), Dan Otero. Jim Schneider later bought the store and moved it to 42 South Broadway in 1996, then sold it in 1997 to James Dovali, who renamed it Relatively Wilde. It closed in 2000. (Photograph by Phil Nash.)

BAKER NEIGHBORHOOD BECOMES BROADWAY TERRACE. In the 1970s, Capitol Hill's reputation as Denver's gayest neighborhood was well established, and real estate became pricier, causing realtors and other entrepreneurs to seek out the next booming "gayborhood." Parts of the Baker neighborhood, roughly south of Sixth Avenue to Alameda Avenue on both sides of Broadway, became known as Broadway Terrace. In the late 1970s and early 1980s, lower home prices along with a cluster of unique gay-owned shops helped lure LGBTQ folks to the area, along with colorful pedestrian traffic. (Photograph by Phil Nash)

WHERE THE GAY WEST PARTIES. Nearly a quarter-century before the film *Brokeback Mountain* popularized the image of the gay cowboy, Charlie's Denver began building a large and loyal clientele of those who appreciate traditional Western style. Opened in August 1981 by owner Jon King (back row, far right) first in the 7000 block of East Colfax Avenue, the bar later moved farther west to 900 East Colfax in the heart of Denver's LGBTQ-friendly Capitol Hill neighborhood. Since its earliest years, Charlie's has been the unofficial headquarters of the Colorado Gay Rodeo Association. (Photograph by Phil Nash.)

ROCKY MOUNTAIN RAINBEAUS. In the early 1980s, with the nearly instant popularity of gay rodeo and all things cowboy, gay square dancing was part of the mix. The Mile High Squares, pictured here, formed in 1981 as part of the Colorado Gay Rodeo Association (CGRA). By 1984, some group members broke off to form the Rocky Mountain Rainbeaus to focus specifically on square dancing. Mile High Squares disbanded by the early 1990s, while the Rainbeaus have thrived over four decades with both male and female members as well as a drag component—the Rainbelles. (Photograph by Phil Nash.)

THE GAY COWBOY WAY. Founded in 1981, the Colorado Gay Rodeo Association was organized to elevate the image of women and men in the sport of rodeo and to promote the country/western lifestyle. Now the nation's longest continuous LGBTQ rodeo organization, CGRA attracts both those raised with rural Western backgrounds and urban enthusiasts of Western traditions and styles. (Photograph by Phil Nash.)

BUNKHOUSE COWBOY FASHION PLATE. Long before *Brokeback Mountain*, Adam Rudziewicz, then co-operator of the Bunkhouse gay guest lodge in Breckenridge, masters the early-1980s gay cowboy look at one of the first Colorado Gay Rodeo Association events. Rudziewicz became the sole owner of the Bunkhouse, which opened in 1972, after his business partner, Rudy Gardner, succumbed to AIDS around 1990. The Bunkhouse passed to new owner Mitch Ringquist after Rudziewicz's death in 2015. (Photograph by Phil Nash.)

DENVER GAY MEN'S CHORUS DEBUT. The San Francisco Gay Men's Chorus, founded in 1978, sparked a nationwide movement to bring gay musicians—and gay-themed music—out of the closet and into performance halls. The Denver Gay Men's Chorus (DGMC) was organized in early 1982 and a few months later kicked off Lesbian and Gay Pride Weekend with its inaugural performance "From The Silence," featuring 74 singers under the direction of founding director Robert Moore. The concert was held at the vintage Aladdin Theatre near East Colfax Avenue and Race Street (now demolished) with 1,300 people attending the two performances. DGMC followed up with sold-out holiday performances later that year. In its inaugural year, the DGMC went on to sing at

the Gay Games in San Francisco and at Lincoln Center in New York for the first GALA Concert festival. The chorus sang for many funerals and memorials of its members as the HIV/AIDS crisis continued to ravage their ranks. DGMC, in turn, inspired choral director Carol White to form the Denver Women's Chorus (DWC) in 1984 and the mixed-voice choral group Harmony in the early 1990s. With the mission of "building community through music," both DGMC and DWC continue to perform to large audiences across metropolitan Denver, operating within the nonprofit Rocky Mountain Arts Association. (Photograph by Phil Nash.)

ROBERT "BOB" MOORE, DGMC DIRECTOR.
Maryland native Bob "Melba" Moore spent much of his life in service to the DGMC, playing many roles including founder, director, codirector, accompanist, and singer. A written tribute states, "Ultimately, with an amazing sense of humility and grace, he settled into the 'grande dame' support role many remember him for." In his later years, he was involved in Sage Singers, a choral group for LGBTQ older adults. Moore died in 2021 at the age of 78. (Photograph by Phil Nash.)

LIFTING SPIRITS WITH MUSIC. At the 1984 national PFLAG convention in Denver, Carol White conducts a mixed-voice chorus of 70 women and 70 men, a feat that would lead to the founding of the Denver Women's Chorus and, several years later, another mixed chorus called Harmony. Although White held two master's degrees in music from Southern Methodist University, she earned her living as a court reporter after the church that employed her dismissed her for being a lesbian. White was a leader in PFLAG Denver and an energetic proponent of building community through music. (Photograph by Phil Nash.)

MILE HIGH FREEDOM BAND, 1985. Controversy erupted in March 1984 when St. Patrick's Day Parade organizers denied an openly gay contingent's permission to participate in the popular annual event in Downtown Denver. The discriminatory policy led recently elected mayor Federico Peña to cancel his appearance to demonstrate support for the LGBTQ community. The following year, the St. Patrick's Day organizers quietly relented, and the recently organized Mile High Freedom Band marched in the parade without incident. Mile High Freedom Bands have expanded over the years to several bands with more than 150 performers. (Photograph by Phil Nash.)

METROPOLITAN COMMUNITY CHURCH (MCC) OF THE ROCKIES. After several years of owning a church at Bannock Street and Evans Avenue, MCC of the Rockies chose to return to Capitol Hill. It purchased this church at Tenth Avenue and Clarkson Street for $500,000 in 1986. Built in the early 1900s, the abandoned building was in serious disrepair. It came to life again over several years as parishioners lovingly restored it, including its original stained-glass windows and an organ rebuilt from original parts. MCC of the Rockies celebrated its golden anniversary in 2023. (Photograph by Phil Nash.)

BALLPARK HEALTH CLUB. Early gay bathhouses hinted at sleaze and shame, often just locker rooms with showers, steam rooms, and shabby cubicles. The Ballpark, opened in 1977 at Bayaud Avenue and Broadway, was a pride-inspiring pleasure palace featuring a pool filled by a waterfall, a vapor cave, and a Mack truck cab—a must-visit attraction for many gay travelers. Unfortunately, bathhouses enabled transmission of HIV before and during the early years of AIDS, attracting public scrutiny to enterprises catering to gay men seeking casual sex. Ultimately, a landlord dispute led to the Ballpark's closing in 1986. (Courtesy of Christi Layne/Christopher Sloan.)

THE EMPIRE BATHS. Opened in the 1970s, the Empire Baths at 6923 East Colfax Avenue closed in 1986 within a month of the Ballpark's closing. According to an article in *Out Front*, the Empire faced an exorbitant increase in the cost of liability insurance due to its operation of two pools—one indoors and another in an enclosed outdoor patio. The facility was later resurrected as the Denver Swim Club, which operated until it was shuttered in 2020 during the COVID-19 pandemic. The Midtowne Spa, another gay bathhouse at Zuni Street near Thirtieth Avenue, also closed during the pandemic. (Courtesy of Christi Layne/Christopher Sloan.)

ALL-NIGHT WAREHOUSE PARTIES. Nightflight was one of a series of all-night warehouse parties held in Denver during the late 1970s and early 1980s. Usually held in abandoned industrial warehouse sites in obscure parts of the city, organizers cleared space for a huge dance floor, brought in top-notch sound systems, hired celebrity DJs, and offered a buffet and beverages to help fuel the dancing mob throughout the night. While the events were alcohol-free, it was common knowledge that most revelers were high on something. (Courtesy of Phil Nash.)

CLUB POSTER, 1942. Opened in 1976, the 1942—and usually just "the '42"—was one of the most popular gay men's bars of the late 1970s and early 1980s. Located at 1942 Broadway near several other gay bars, the 1942's ads projected the image of the gay male "types" it was trying to attract as customers—leather men, cowboys, and pumped-up jocks. At one point, the club was accused of turning away men of color, which drew anti-racism pickets. (Courtesy of History Colorado.)

GAY GAMES TORCH RUN, 1982. An Olympic-style torch run across the United States helped build excitement for the inaugural Gay Games in San Francisco. A group of Denver gay bicyclists carried the torch over Berthoud Pass, elevation 11,307 feet, the highest point of the torch's journey across the country. (Photograph by Phil Nash.)

DENVER'S EARLIEST GAY SOCCER LEAGUE. Inspired by the first Gay Games in 1982, a number of gay and lesbian sports groups, such as this gay men's soccer group, began to form throughout the 1980s, offering healthy social alternatives to gay nightlife. Today, Team Colorado is an umbrella organization that serves as a connecting point for individuals interested in individual and team athletics ranging from biking to wrestling. (Photograph by Phil Nash.)

LESBIAN VISIBILITY IN WOMEN'S MOVEMENT. The women's liberation movement of the 1970s was initially chilly to visible lesbian participation, even though lesbians had been leaders of the women's movement since at least suffragette days. In this undated photograph, workers from the collective household of Woman to Woman Book Center and *Big Mama Rag* newspaper made this banner to carry at an International Women's Day March. (Courtesy of History Colorado.)

PLATTE VALLEY WATERING HOLE. The Fox Hole was one of Denver's most popular and enduring bars from the late 1970s until the early 2000s, when it was inevitably closed and eventually scraped as the Central Platte Valley was developed into a new residential neighborhood. In 2003, *Westword* honored the Fox Hole with a Best of Denver award, stating that the bar "deserves to be made a national historic landmark. We've danced to the rhythm under that giant cottonwood tree through two economic booms, three busts, a sports-bar name change and a complete neighborhood transformation." (Photograph by Phil Nash.)

ALEXANDER FOUNDATION BOOSTS LGBTQ PHILANTHROPY. Founded in 1981 by University of Denver political science professor Bill Leavel, the Alexander Foundation raises funds to support LGBTQ people in need and provide scholarships. The organization was named after the ancient Macedonian conqueror Alexander the Great, who was said to love men. This photograph was taken in about 1992 at a fundraiser held at Neiman Marcus. Pictured from left to right are Bob Asmus, Bill Leavel (founder), Jay Swope, Jeffrey Ziese, Elizabeth Bryant, Katherine Peck, Chuck Schilling, Barbara Harrison, Ron Penn, an unidentified woman, Gary Sky, and Kent Epperson. (Photograph by David Ford.)

Five

THERE IS NO TURNING BACK

By the early 1980s, Denver's "Cowtown" reputation had waned. In the 1970s, tens of thousands of baby boomers moved to Colorado enchanted by John Denver's "Rocky Mountain High" and the thrill of skiing. The in-migration included many young LGBTQ urban pioneers who settled into historic but neglected neighborhoods near Downtown Denver—Capitol Hill, Baker, Congress Park, Uptown—and began transforming them into LGBTQ-friendly urban villages.

A political makeover was also in the works. By 1983's city elections, Mayor Bill McNichols had held office for 15 years and was running for another four-year term. But Denver's changing demographics disrupted his plans. That spring, a barely known two-term Latino legislator from West Denver named Federico Peña tapped into a groundswell of voters seeking change. His campaign slogan, "Imagine a Great City," heralded a new era. Propelled by hundreds of volunteers, Peña defeated six other candidates, including McNichols, thanks to his inclusive message that built a powerful coalition of Latino, Black, women, labor, pro-environment, and LGBTQ voters.

City hall's doors opened to the LGBTQ community. Peña appointed an open lesbian as his liaison to the community. He and his team began meeting with LGBTQ leaders to hear concerns and then initiate changes. Discriminatory policing ended. LGBTQ people joined advisory groups to help move Peña's transformational agenda forward. A dynamic speaker, Peña generously lent his celebrity status to LGBTQ and AIDS fundraising events. Perhaps most important, Peña's victories in 1983 and his 1987 reelection demonstrated to other politicians that LGBTQ voters could sway elections. In years to come, a growing number of politicians appeared in Pride parades seeking visibility with LGBTQ voters.

Peña was not the first Denver politician to support LGBTQ issues. US representative Pat Schroeder; statehouse legislators Wellington Webb and Jack McCroskey; and Denver's first two Denver City councilwomen, Cathy Reynolds and Cathy Donohue, were going to bat for the LGBTQ community. But after Peña, no candidate for office in Denver could succeed without seeking LGBTQ support. Empowered with greater access to the levers of city government, activists began the long march toward ensuring equal rights for Denver's LGBTQ citizens.

FED UP WITH THE MAYOR. Denver mayor Bill McNichols (who served 1968–1983) never tried to make friends with the lesbian and gay community. After twice turning down eligible grant funding for the Gay Community Center of Colorado, after years of looking the other way as the Denver vice squad trampled on the rights of gay, lesbian, and transgender citizens, and showing no willingness to acknowledge the community's concerns, LGBTQ activists launched the "Dump McNichols" campaign during the 1979 city elections. He was reelected that year but defeated four years later. (Photograph by Phil Nash.)

PROTESTING GAY BAR DISCRIMINATION. The 1942 Club, a popular dance bar for the Levi's crowd in the late 1970s and early 1980s, reportedly began screening patrons at the door, requiring as many as three pieces of picture ID for Black patrons seeking admission while only requiring the usual one piece of ID for white patrons. The practice essentially excluded Blacks from the club. When word got around, LGBTQ anti-racism activists picketed and called for a boycott. The man in front is unidentified. Pictured in the second row are, from left to right, two unidentified persons, Patrick Gourley, Jim Dennison, and Donaciano Martinez. (Photograph by Phil Nash.)

HARRY HAY AND RADICAL FAERIES. In August 1980, Colorado was the site of the second Spiritual Gathering for Radical Faeries in the Pike–San IsabelNational Forest near Pine, Colorado. Harry Hay (second from left), who cofounded the Mattachine Society in 1950, was a cofounder of the radical faerie movement and built relationships with a Denver-based group to organize the large outdoor gathering. Hay exhorted 200-plus attendees to "throw off the ugly green frogskin of hetero-imitation to find the shining Faerie prince beneath." Faerie circles were organized at the conference on subjects as varied as massage, nutrition, healing energy, "gay enspiritment," and more. (Photograph by Phil Nash.)

MURALS AT BJ'S CAROUSEL. Established by Bob Engel and partner John Neugebauer ("B" and "J") in 1977, BJ's Carousel, at 1380 South Broadway, was one of the most popular and longest-lived gay bars in Denver. It offered drag shows, a small restaurant, a piano, and a fenced-in volleyball "beach." Artist Charlie Donalson created murals surrounding BJ's outdoor area depicting BJ's eclectic mix of customers. Engel was a founding board member of the Colorado AIDS Project (now Colorado Health Network) and helped raise more than $750,000 for the organization over two decades at BJ's annual Carousel Ball. BJ's closed in 2011. (Photograph by Phil Nash.)

Two Cathys Advance Gay Rights. In 1975, Cathy Donohue (above) and Cathy Reynolds were the first two women elected to Denver City Council; Reynolds held an at-large seat for a city record of 28-plus years until 2003, while Donohue represented District 10 in central Denver until 1995, when she joined the Wellington Webb mayoral administration. Donohue, initially considered a feisty outsider, was an ally from the start and always enjoyed strong gay community support. While in office, she availed herself to help individuals and organizations navigate city bureaucracies. She later served on the board of the Gay and Lesbian Community Center. Reynolds, initially chilly to the community, became a fierce champion in the 1980s, leading efforts to eliminate discriminatory "families only" zoning restrictions in some neighborhoods and pass a comprehensive human rights ordinance in 1990. (Above, photograph by Phil Nash; left, photograph by David Ford.)

FEDERICO PEÑA ELECTED MAYOR. Denver's 1983 municipal election ushered in a new era when 36-year-old Federico Peña was elected mayor, defeating the 16-year incumbent Bill McNichols. Campaigning with the optimistic slogan "Imagine a Great City," Peña built a coalition of Hispanics, Blacks, women, LGBTQ people, and labor and other groups that were eager for Denver to move on from its cowtown roots and build for the future. Endorsed by *Out Front* and supported by many LGBTQ activists, Peña opened city hall's doors to LGBTQ concerns and encouraged LGBTQ involvement in city government. Peña served two terms, leaving office in 1991. (Photograph by Phil Nash.)

PEÑA APPOINTS LIAISON. After winning his dark-horse campaign for mayor in 1983, Denver mayor Federico Peña appointed open lesbian Carol Hunt as his liaison to the LGBTQ community to ensure open communication between his administration and the community through the Commission on Community Relations (now called the Office of Human Rights and Community Partnerships). Hunt was the first known open LGBTQ mayoral appointment in the Denver city government. She held the position throughout Peña's eight years in office, helping LGBTQ and HIV/AIDS organizations navigate city government and bringing awareness of LGBTQ concerns to city departments. (Photograph by Phil Nash.)

COMING OUT OUTDOORS. By the early 1980s, two groups had formed to encourage lesbians and gay men to engage in outdoor recreation as a healthy alternative to gay nightlife. Dee Farrell, left, was a leader in the Women's Outdoor Club, which taught participants new skills, offered outdoor activities, and offered ways to meet like-minded friends. Howard Cole was a cofounder of The Group, which organized diverse outdoor recreational activities and social events for gay men. In this 1983 photograph, Farrell and Cole preside over a joint get-together of the Women's Outdoor Club and The Group. (Photograph by David Ford.)

FESTIVE TIME ON THE SLOPES. Among other activities, The Group organized ski trips to enjoy Colorado's favorite outdoor pastime, occasionally with a flourish of camp. These high-kicking Rockettes imitators from a 1982 trip are, from left to right, Ron Sanford, Rick ?, Lynne Pettigrew, and Kevin Elandt. (The man in the rear is unidentified.) In the 1990s, The Group's name changed to the FrontRangers. (Photograph by David Ford.)

ROCKY MOUNTAINEERS AT THE
TRIANGLE. Founded in 1968, the
Rocky Mountaineers Motorcycle
Club's headquarters were at the
Triangle Lounge, 2036 Broadway,
a bar for the leather and Levi's
crowd from the 1970s to the early
2000s. RMMC was the oldest
gay organization in Colorado
and remained active for about
45 years, disbanding in 2014 as
membership dwindled. RMMC
held an annual calendar of
motorcycle runs, most of which
began and ended at the Triangle.
The Triangle underwent several
transformations over the decades
before closing in 2023, fifty years
after it first opened as a gay leather
bar. (Photograph by Bill Olson.)

TEN IMPERIAL EMPRESSES. In the
mid-1980s, ten of the first twelve
Empresses of the Imperial Court of
the Rocky Mountain Empire gathered
at the stepping-down ceremony for
Empress XII Jamie Cole (first row,
center). Jamie is flanked by Stephanie
McCall (VII), left, and Jaye Sutherland
(XI), right. The others are, from left
to right, (second row) Causha Lee
Victoria (IV), Vaden Andress (IX),
Annie Brenman-West (VIII), and
Christi Layne Elizabeth (VI); (third
row) Billie Cassandra (III), Bridgette
Peters (I), and Scotti Carlyle (II). Not
pictured are Mikel Wright (V) and
Brandy Dennison (X). (Courtesy of
Christi Layne/Christopher Sloan.)

GAY GAMES, 1986. The Denver-based Colorado Athletic Exchange (CAE) organized more than 100 LGBTQ competitors in a variety of sports to attend the Second International Gay Games in San Francisco from August 10 to 17, 1986. This photograph shows the Colorado contingent getting ready to march in the opening ceremonies wearing their blue warm-up suits. Originally named the Gay Olympics when the first event was held in 1982, the name was changed to the Gay Games after the US Olympic Committee won a lawsuit at the US Supreme Court restricting the use of

"Olympics." Participation grew from 1,350 in 1982 to 3,500 in 1986 to more than 13,000 at the 2018 Paris Gay Games 10. The Federation of Gay Games is an international organization with a mission to "promote equality, diversity and inclusion through sport and culture . . . built on the core principles of participation, inclusion, and personal best . . . open to all, young or old, athlete or artist, experienced or novice, gay or straight." (Photograph by Phil Nash.)

SYNCHRONIZED SWIMWEAR. A half dozen members of the Colorado Athletic Exchange's Denver swim team at the 1986 Gay Games model their chic Speedos emblazoned with the state's iconic red, blue, and yellow colors. In 1992, LGBTQ swimmers formally organized as SQUID—Swimming Queers United In Denver—and welcome swimmers of all abilities and identities. (Photograph by Phil Nash.)

WOMEN'S SOFTBALL AT THE 1990 GAY GAMES. Denver was well represented at the 1990 Gay Games, held August 4 through 11 in Vancouver, British Columbia. In this picture, members of the Denver Women's Softball League are enjoying some antics between games. (Photograph by David Ford.)

CENTER VOLUNTEERS RALLY. As the Gay and Lesbian Community Center approached its 10th anniversary in the mid-1980s, it faced challenges in leadership and funding. By that time, fundraising for AIDS organizations had eclipsed efforts to support the center, and for a short time, the center became an all-volunteer organization without stable office space. In a public demonstration of support for the organization's survival, volunteers gathered for a group portrait at the Cheesman Park Pavilion. While some programs were curtailed, others took root, and the organization survived and regained strength in the late 1980s. (Photograph by Phil Nash.)

EQUAL PROTECTION ORDINANCE COALITION (EPOC). Tea Schook was a leader in EPOC's efforts to modify Denver's R-0 zoning to allow more than one unmarried person to cohabit in a residence in areas zoned R-0, a violation often enforced against same-sex couples but not unmarried heterosexuals. EPOC then advocated at Denver City Council to pass a comprehensive human rights ordinance including sexual orientation in 1990. This provoked a conservative political initiative, in May 1991, to delete "sexual orientation" from Denver's new ordinance, which voters rejected. Schook, a longtime lesbian and feminist activist, briefly ran for governor in 1990, the first LGBTQ person to do so. (Courtesy of the Center on Colfax.)

Six

FIGHTING FOR OUR LIVES

In July 1981, *Out Front* was the first Colorado publication to report news from the Centers for Disease Control about a rare pneumonia found in a small cluster of previously healthy gay men in Los Angeles. Then news arrived from San Francisco and New York about unusual immune-deficiency diseases among gay men leading to rapid decline and death. Soon, scientists suggested it was sexually transmitted, and Gay-Related Immune Deficiency (GRID) briefly joined the medical lexicon. But other groups were also getting the disease: hemophiliacs, Haitians, and intravenous drug users. By late 1982, the disease was renamed Acquired Immune Deficiency Syndrome (AIDS), but the cause remained elusive. Effective, life-saving treatments would not be available for more than a dozen more years.

Knowing AIDS would reach Colorado, Denver gay activists and healthcare workers began to organize. A new group, the Gay and Lesbian Health Alliance of Denver (GLHAD), began sharing information and planning a community response. The Gay and Lesbian Community Center formed the Colorado AIDS Project (CAP) to develop services. From eight Colorado cases reported in 1982, AIDS diagnoses reached 123 by 1985, with 86 percent of them gay men; 84 people had died. In 1984, CAP was incorporated as a separate nonprofit. Julian Rush, earlier fired from the Methodist ministry after being outed as gay, became CAP's first executive director.

In 1983, GLHAD cosponsored and helped organize the Fifth National Lesbian/Gay Health Conference at Denver's Executive Tower Inn (today the Curtis Hotel), drawing more than 300 North American health professionals. AIDS dominated the agenda, but the meeting's most enduring outcome was the Denver Principles, a stunning manifesto written by 11 gay men with AIDS. The document revolutionized the perception and treatment of people with HIV/AIDS.

Fear and grief engulfed the community into the mid-1990s, when the first effective treatments became available. Thousands of volunteers helped provide services, raise funds, advocate for public policy, and protest the slow, indifferent government response to this deadly public health crisis. Many lesbians, earlier wary of engaging in gay-identified organizations, stepped forward to support and lead them. Culturally appropriate services were organized for nongay risk groups—Black men and women, Latinos, Native Americans, children, and others. The LGBTQ community's strength was tested—and perhaps fortified—as religious extremists condemned AIDS sufferers, claiming the disease was God's punishment for immorality. The ugly spectacle of societal homophobia could no longer be ignored. While the losses were staggering, AIDS catalyzed LGBTQ alliances with healthcare institutions, government entities, foundations, businesses, and a more supportive public.

LEADERSHIP EMERGES TO ADDRESS AIDS EPIDEMIC. Initially a program of the Gay and Lesbian Community Center, the Colorado AIDS Project became an independent nonprofit in 1984. Its early motto was "The Loving Touch of a Caring Community." The photograph is from an early board retreat. Pictured from left to right are (first row) executive director Julian Rush, Jim Nichols, Max Evans, Phil Nash, Donna Cecere, Bruce Rosenberg, and John Jay; (second row) Paul Mesard, Lee Rudofsky, Bob Engel, Tim Timmons, Jill Friedman-Fixler, and Bob Yegge. (Courtesy of the Colorado Health Network.)

HEALTH OFFICIALS CONFRONT AIDS. In the early 1980s, Dr. Thomas Vernon (left), head of the Colorado Department of Health, and Dr. Frank Judson of Denver Public Health, were among the most aggressive public health officials in the nation in attempting to slow the spread of AIDS in the state using contact tracing, a standard epidemiological practice. They drew heated criticism from many AIDS activists who opposed contact tracing as a violation of patient confidentiality. (Photograph by Phil Nash.)

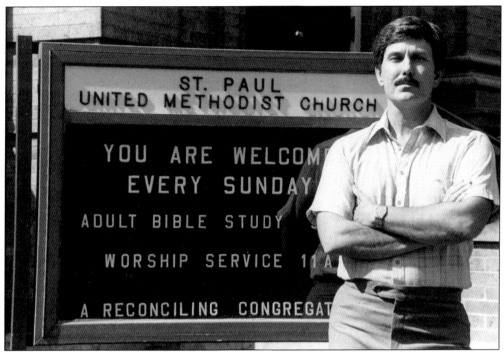

OPENLY GAY MINISTER STIRS NATIONAL CONTROVERSY. When the Reverend Julian Rush came out to his senior pastor at the Boulder United Methodist Church in 1981, he was fired, dividing the congregation and making national news. Bishop Melvin Wheatley, who championed the rights of lesbian and gay Methodist ministers, later appointed Rush pastor of central Denver's St. Paul's United Methodist Church. Rush also became the first director of the Colorado AIDS Project, which he saw as another way to further his spiritual vocation. (Photograph by Phil Nash.)

ST. PAUL'S UNITED METHODIST CHURCH. In the 1980s, the United Methodist Church began a decades-long debate over the role of LGBT people in the church. St. Paul's UMC congregation at Sixteenth Avenue and Ogden Street had dwindled over time, but when it became an early welcoming and affirming congregation for LGBT people, its fortunes turned around. St. Paul's donated office space for the Colorado AIDS Project in its formative stage. Today, the stately building is home to Belong Church, with a focus on social justice. (Photograph by Phil Nash.)

THE DENVER PRINCIPLES. At the 1983 Gay and Lesbian Health Conference, "Health Pioneering in the 80s," held in Denver, 11 men with AIDS presented a manifesto demanding just and humane treatment for people with AIDS. Known as the Denver Principles, their document has been influential worldwide in the care and treatment of people with HIV and AIDS. From left to right are (first row) Phil Lanzarratta, Rich Berkowitz, Tom Nasrallah, Mathew Sarner, Bobby Reynolds, and Artie Felson; (second row) Bill Burke, Dan Turner, Mike Callen, Bobbi Campbell, and Bob Checci. As of 2023, only author and advocate Berkowitz was still known to be living. (Photograph by John Schoenwalter.)

HONORING THE DENVER PRINCIPLES. On June 12, 2023, organizations serving people with HIV/AIDS gathered to recognize the 40th anniversary of the creation of the Denver Principles at the Curtis Hotel, where the manifesto was first presented in June 1983. People living with HIV took turns reading the historic document. The readers are, from left to right, Kari Perry, Robert Riester, Kalvin Gipson, Miguel Landers, Barb Cardell, Mary Jane Maestas, Jadyn Sloan, and Fernando Macias. (Photograph by Phil Nash.)

PEOPLE WITH AIDS HAVE THE RIGHT:

- to have full explanations of all medical procedures and risks

- to refuse to participate in treatment research without jeopardizing treatment

- to privacy, to confidentiality of all medical records, to human respect

- to quality medical treatment and social service provisions without discrimination due to sexual orientation, diagnosis, economic status, race

- to be included in every level of decision making of AIDS groups

- to an advocate to ask questions on their behalf

- to choose who their significant others are and to have them treated with the same respect as others while visiting in the hospital

- to be treated by hospital staff who are accurately informed about gay health care issues as well as AIDS

- to as full and satisfying sexual and emotional lives as anyone else

PRINCIPLES IN PRACTICE. This panel from an early Colorado AIDS Project brochure (1983 or 1984) concisely states the key points of the manifesto written only months earlier by the authors of the Denver Principles. These fundamental ideas have informed treatment of and services for people with HIV/AIDS ever since. (Courtesy of Phil Nash.)

PEOPLE WITH AIDS SHARE STORIES. While most people with AIDS (PWAs) shunned public attention, a few stepped forward to talk about living with AIDS. Mikel Wright, Empress V of the Imperial Court and well known in many Denver gay circles, was among the earliest AIDS cases in Colorado. In a March 1984 interview with *Out Front*, Wright spoke of his response to his diagnosis: "I wasn't going to just roll over and die. Too often PWAs . . . give up and say, 'Why bother?' My belief system doesn't work that way. If you have a day, use it." Wright died in 1985. (Photograph by Phil Nash.)

RESEARCH RIVALS MEET IN DENVER. Dr. Luc Montagnier (left) of France's Pasteur Institute and Dr. Robert Gallo of the US National Institutes of Health each took credit for discovering the virus that causes AIDS. Much was at stake, including patents and professional reputations. Tensions between the international rivals were subdued at a 1985 Denver conference on AIDS sponsored by AMC Cancer Research Center and Hospital. Years later, it was determined that the French had identified the human immunodeficiency virus (HIV) a year before their US counterparts. (Photograph by Phil Nash.)

PROTESTING RELIGIOUS BIGOTRY. In June 1983, as the AIDS epidemic surged, Moral Majority founder Rev. Jerry Falwell told his followers that "AIDS is not just God's punishment for homosexuals, it is God's punishment for the society that tolerates homosexuals." Falwell's outsize influence on politics and the media brutally stigmatized LGBTQ people and slowed the allocation of public dollars to address the epidemic. When Falwell spoke at the Colorado State Capitol in the mid-1980s, he attracted more than a thousand protestors, including Donaciano Martinez, who is kissing his friend Kevin Barlow. (Photograph by Phil Nash.)

ARTIST SHARES RESPONSE TO AIDS. Artist and activist Roger Beltrami created *Skeletons Protesting the Indifference of the Reagan Administration to Gay Men with AIDS* as commentary on the federal government's silence and inaction to the HIV/AIDS epidemic. The skeletons carried the slogans "Silence=Death" and "Action=Life" used by ACT UP (AIDS Coalition to Unleash Power) in its confrontational, nonviolent protests. Beltrami, along with Rex Fuller and Scott Little, organized ACT UP Colorado in 1988, putting pressure on state and local governments to increase AIDS funding and ban discrimination against people living with HIV/AIDS. (Courtesy of History Colorado.)

MAYOR SUPPORTS EARLY FUNDRAISING RACE. Soon after his 1983 election, Mayor Federico Peña invited individuals involved in AIDS work to provide a briefing for him at his office. In this picture, Ray Kemble (left) and Jeff Logan present the mayor with a t-shirt with the numeral 1 for "Torches in the Wind," a foot race to benefit the Colorado AIDS Project. An avid runner himself, Peña often lent his celebrity status to promote physical fitness and his clout to close streets to accommodate large races. (Photograph by Phil Nash.)

AIDS WALK COLORADO. Over the years, AIDS Walk Colorado has been one of the largest outdoor fundraisers in the state. First organized in the late 1980s, the AIDS Walk provided a way for thousands of people from all walks of life to get involved in supporting services for people with AIDS and, later, those living with HIV. This 1992 photograph of the AIDS Walk registration table shows the high level of organization needed to handle the enthusiastic crowds. Today, proceeds from AIDS Walk Colorado benefit the Colorado Health Network. (Photograph by David Ford.)

WOMEN AND AIDS. The Empowerment Program, founded in 1986, helps remove barriers to health, housing, education, and employment so individuals can live healthier lives. Serving primarily cis and transgender women who have lived experiences with the criminal legal system or homelessness, Empowerment has worked with many women living with HIV and AIDS. Carol Lease, right, a former executive director of the Gay and Lesbian Community Center, later cofounder and executive director of Empowerment, is pictured with her team walking to raise funds for HIV/AIDS in 1993. (Photograph by David Ford.)

PROJECT ANGEL HEART. When Charles Robbins (left) returned to Denver from Los Angeles in 1991, he witnessed friends living with HIV/AIDS wasting away, so he founded Project Angel Heart (PAH), modeled after Los Angeles's Project Angel Food, where he had volunteered. Initially, Robbins and friends solicited food from restaurants to deliver on weekends, but with increasing demand, they moved into the kitchen of St. Barnabas Episcopal Church and started cooking. PAH continued to grow and, over time, expanded its scope to provide "food as medicine" to people experiencing serious illnesses. (Photograph by David Ford.)

EARLY **AIDS** OFFICE. Quickly outgrowing donated office space in the mid-1980s, the Colorado AIDS Project rented space at 1577 Clarkson Street. Within two years, this building also became obsolete as the client load and programs multiplied. (Photograph by Phil Nash.)

AIDS PROJECT HEADQUARTERS. This building on the northeast corner of East Colfax Avenue and Washington Street is today the Denver Police Department's District 6 headquarters. The boxy 1960s-era structure, formerly a medical clinic, served as CAP's headquarters in the late 1980s and early 1990s. CAP later moved to the Diamond Hill office complex in northwest Denver, where it remained until it conducted a capital campaign to buy its own building. (Photograph by Phil Nash.)

ORGANIZATION PROVIDES STATEWIDE **HIV/AIDS** SERVICES. The Colorado Health Network's roots go back to 1983, when the Gay and Lesbian Community Center launched the Colorado AIDS Project. CAP became independent in 1984, serving primarily metro Denver. Independent AIDS organizations developed in various regions of Colorado, with four of them consolidating in 2011 under the rebranded administrative umbrella Colorado Health Network (CHN). CHN purchased and remodeled a former Woolworth's department store in east Denver as its headquarters, later also adding dental and medical services tailored to people with HIV. (Photograph by Phil Nash.)

HOUSING FOR PEOPLE WITH **AIDS/HIV.** In the early years of AIDS, many PWAs faced a housing crisis if they could not work, often because of housing discrimination due to unjustified fears. Opened in 1996, the Chesney-Kleinjohn apartment building at Tenth Street and Washington Avenue helped fill the housing gap and today continues to accommodate low-income people living with HIV. (Photograph by Phil Nash.)

COLORADO AIDS MEMORIAL. Realtor Doug McNeil died of AIDS in 1993, asking close friends to help establish an AIDS memorial in Denver. In collaboration with Denver Parks, on August 12, 2000, a natural riverside area in Commons Park was established as The Grove "dedicated to the remembrance of those who have lost their lives to AIDS and to their loving caregivers who helped them live out those lives with dignity and grace." Located near Fifteenth and Little Raven Streets on the banks of the South Platte River, The Grove was rededicated in 2016. This group of volunteers came to help spruce up the area. (Courtesy of Phil Nash.)

FOUR DECADES OF CARING COMPASSION. The Colorado Health Network, formerly known as the Colorado AIDS Project, celebrated its 40th anniversary in September 2023. Colorado's oldest and largest nonprofit serving people living with HIV, Denver-based CHN operates programs in Colorado Springs, Fort Collins, Greeley, Grand Junction, and Pueblo. From left to right are client services manager Robert Riester, CEO Darrell Vigil, chief clinical officer Lili Carrillo, and chief programs officer Jamie Villalobos. (Photograph by Phil Nash.)

Seven

AMENDMENT 2 AND THE "HATE STATE"

By the late 1980s, LGBTQ progress sparked a backlash among religious conservatives both in Denver and statewide. In 1991, Denver voters soundly defeated conservative-led Initiative 1 to delete sexual orientation from the comprehensive civil rights ordinance passed by the Denver City Council in 1990. In conservative Colorado Springs, Colorado for Family Values (CFV) formed as a political advocacy group to stop gay rights from progressing to the national stage. CFV's message was amplified by popular University of Colorado football coach Bill McCartney, founder of Promise Keepers, a Christian men's movement. CFV succeeded in getting an antigay constitutional amendment on the November 3, 1992, ballot. Amendment 2 would nullify existing sexual orientation discrimination protections in Denver, Boulder, and Aspen and forbid future state or local protections.

Pre-election polls forecasted Amendment 2's defeat, but it passed with 53.41 percent of the vote. Analysts credited CFV's victory on the misleading claim that gay rights were "special rights." The news came as a shock, with Colorado being branded "the hate state" and with a national Boycott Colorado campaign leading to an estimated $40 million in lost visitor revenue and cancellations of appearances by celebrity performers. Within weeks, Richard Evans, a gay Denver city employee, filed suit against Amendment 2. A local judge issued an injunction until the lawsuit was adjudicated. In 1994, the Colorado Supreme Court ruled it unconstitutional, and the boycott ended. The state appealed to the US Supreme Court in the case known as *Romer v. Evans*. On May 20, 1996, the Supreme Court upheld the lower court's decision by a vote of 6-3. Amendment 2 never went into effect.

EPOColorado (Equal Protection Ordinance Colorado), the organization that advocated for Denver's human rights ordinance and successfully defeated the initiative to strip "sexual orientation" from it, stepped up to organize the statewide "No on 2" campaign.

Financing and managing a statewide political campaign took a huge toll on a community already tapped out from fighting AIDS. It would take even more money to support the Colorado Legal Initiatives Project (CLIP), which was formed to fight Amendment 2 at the US Supreme Court. As LGBTQ and allied donors shifted to fund this extended political emergency, other priorities in the LGBTQ community were sidelined. But the crisis birthed a new form of gay activism: large-scale philanthropy. After Amendment 2 passed, gay Denver tech entrepreneur Tim Gill announced a $1-million gift to overturn it. "The Gill Foundation is one of the results of my getting pissed off about Amendment 2," Gill says in his oral history for the LGBTQ History Project at the Center on Colfax. The Gill Foundation helped shore up struggling LGBTQ nonprofits locally and launched initiatives across Colorado and the nation to advance LGBTQ rights.

STATE CAPITOL RALLY AGAINST AMENDMENT 2. The 1992 campaign to defeat Amendment 2 mobilized the Colorado LGBTQ community like nothing before. This time, efforts to defeat the measure drew legions of nongay allies to the cause. The effort by Colorado for Family Values to exclude LGBTQ Coloradans from constitutional antidiscrimination protections was a clarion call to resist the mounting influence of religious conservatives to enact laws and policies that would make LGBTQ people permanent second-class citizens. (Courtesy of History Colorado.)

GOV. ROY ROMER. A stalwart supporter of LGBTQ rights, Gov. Roy Romer (served 1987–1999) sports a "No on 2" campaign button during the Fall 1992 campaign season, signaling his opposition to Amendment 2. Ironically, after Amendment 2 passed, his name was associated with the US Supreme Court lawsuit because, in his official role, Romer was obligated to uphold the will of a majority of Colorado voters. Romer and his wife, Bea, had been involved in civil rights activism decades earlier over race-based housing discrimination in Denver's Park Hill neighborhood. (Photograph by David Ford.)

CELEBRITIES SUPPORT NO ON 2. Tennis champion Martina Navratilova (above, left) and comedian/actress Lily Tomlin show off their No on 2 t-shirts when they were in Denver for a high-dollar fundraising event to defeat Amendment 2. Navratilova was outed as bisexual in the early 1980s and later identified publicly as lesbian. Tomlin's lesbianism was an open secret in Hollywood, which she did not discuss publicly until her mother's death in 2005. At right, EPOColorado assistant campaign manager Joseph Marchione (left) is pictured with esteemed British actor Sir Ian McKellen, who came out publicly in 1988 to protest Prime Minister Margaret Thatcher's antigay policies. Knighted by Queen Elizabeth II in 1991, McKellen lent his star power to the No on 2 campaign at a press conference and fundraising luncheon to defeat the antigay initiative. Marchione donated dozens of EPOColorado photographs to History Colorado. (Both, courtesy of History Colorado.)

LGBTQ ATTORNEYS ORGANIZE. The Colorado Lesbian Gay Law Association (CLGLA) was formed in early 1992. Later that year, CLGLA chair Milo Gonser (right) presented a check from the group to Judy Harrington, campaign manager of the No on 2 campaign to help defeat Amendment 2. The organization is today known as the Colorado LGBT Bar Association. (Courtesy of History Colorado.)

TENSE ELECTION NIGHT. On November 3, 1992, the staff and volunteers for Equal Protection Ordinance Colorado spent a heartbreaking evening in their office as the election returns began to show insurmountable support for Amendment 2's passage. Pictured here are Tina Scardina (right), one of EPOColorado's key leaders, and Richard Evans, a Denver city employee who became the lead plaintiff in *Romer v. Evans*, the case that went to the US Supreme Court. Scardina served in Mayor Wellington Webb's administration as a liaison to the LGBTQ community and staffed the newly launched LGBTQ Commission, which Webb formed soon after taking office. (Courtesy of History Colorado.)

COLORADO LEGAL INITIATIVES PROJECT. In the weeks leading up to the November 1992 election, a group of lawyers and activists began meeting quietly to formulate "Plan B"—what to do if Amendment 2 passed. Immediately after Amendment 2 passed, the Colorado Legal Initiatives Project went public with a plan to challenge its constitutionality. Like the EPOColorado campaign to defeat Amendment 2, it would require significant private fundraising, while the State of Colorado would defend Amendment 2 with taxpayer dollars. After Amendment 2 was declared unconstitutional by the US Supreme Court, CLIP was transformed into the legal services program at the Center on Colfax. (Courtesy of History Colorado.)

MARCH ON WASHINGTON, 1993. On April 25, 1993, an estimated one million people joined the March on Washington for Lesbian, Gay, and Bi Equal Rights and Liberation, the largest-ever protest in the nation's capital to that date. With the November 1992 passage of Colorado's Amendment 2, the national call to action was more urgent than ever, as voters across the country might follow Colorado in voting for state constitutional roadblocks to LGBTQ equality. As the first state threatened with the loss of antidiscrimination protections, Colorado was dubbed "Ground Zero" in a nationwide effort by conservatives to roll back progress toward LGBTQ equality. The US Supreme Court overruled Amendment 2 on May 20, 1996. (Photograph by Phil Nash.)

ONWARD TO THE SUPREME COURT. Pictured here at a No on 2 rally, longtime lesbian leader Linda Fowler stepped up as one of the plaintiffs in *Romer v. Evans*, the case undertaken by the Colorado Legal Initiatives Project to get Amendment 2 declared unconstitutional by the US Supreme Court. During the previous two decades before Amendment 2, Fowler had been an effective and outspoken organizer in lesbian, women's, and LGBTQ social justice activism, including volunteering with *Big Mama Rag* newspaper, the Lesbians-Colorado conference, and protests against police harassment. (Courtesy of History Colorado.)

GROUP SHOT IN WASHINGTON BEFORE HEARING. Plaintiffs in *Romer v. Evans* and CLIP leaders pose for a group shot with District 1 congresswoman Patricia Schroeder when the group went to observe the US Supreme Court hearings in Washington, DC. Pictured from left to right are Paul Brown, Angela Romero, Patrick Steadman, Linda Fowler, Richard Evans, an unidentified male, Schroeder, Priscilla Inkpen, Leslie Durgan, and Mary Celeste. (Courtesy of Mary Celeste.)

CONGRESSMAN DAVID SKAGGS LENDS SUPPORT. Chief plaintiff Richard Evans, right, greets US representative David Skaggs of House District 2 at a gathering in Washington, DC, when Colorado's delegation went for the US Supreme Court hearing on *Romer v. Evans*. Skaggs's district covered Denver's western and northern suburbs, then considered a swing district. (Courtesy of Mary Celeste.)

AMENDMENT TWO'S DAY IN COURT. Mary Celeste (left), cochair of the Colorado Legal Initiatives Project, and Jean Dubofsky, the lead attorney arguing against Amendment 2, leave the US Supreme Court after oral arguments on October 10, 1995. At 37, Dubofsky had been the first woman and the youngest person appointed to the Colorado Supreme Court, later starting a private practice specializing in appellate law. Dubofsky succeeded in convincing six of the nine justices that Amendment 2 violated the equal protection clause of the 14th Amendment of the US Constitution, ultimately providing the legal basis for same-sex marriage two decades later. (Courtesy of Mary Celeste.)

CELEBRATING THE WIN! By a vote of 6-3, the US Supreme Court declared Amendment 2 unconstitutional on May 20, 1996. After the legal victory, the Colorado Legal Initiatives Project held an appreciation dinner for CLIP volunteers and attorneys. Frank Brown (right), who served as CLIP's executive director, is pictured with Kenny Finger in front of a banner proclaiming "CLIP undid 2!" Brown said that learning that Amendment 2 was unconstitutional was "one of the happiest days of my life." Brown donated dozens of CLIP photographs to History Colorado. (Courtesy of History Colorado.)

BRINGING THE VICTORY HOME. In May 1996, CLIP cochair and cofounder Mary Celeste spoke at the Colorado State Capitol about CLIP's victory at the US Supreme Court after six of the nine justices ruled that Amendment 2 was unconstitutional. It was a joyful moment after LGBTQ Coloradans spent nearly four years in agonizing uncertainty about whether they would be forever relegated to second-class citizenship under the law. (Courtesy of History Colorado.)

BITTERSWEET COMMEMORATIVE GIFT. Despite the painful loss at the polls when Amendment 2 passed, when the campaign was over, volunteers were given a small paperweight emblazoned with the fated campaign's logo. The pink triangle in the logo refers to the symbol that homosexuals were forced to wear while imprisoned in Nazi concentration camps during World War II. The message took on a deeper meaning later when the US Supreme Court essentially said, "No on 2," settling the matter for good. (Photograph by Phil Nash.)

LEADING THROUGH A CRISIS. Kat Morgan served as the executive director of the Gay and Lesbian Community Center in 1992–1993 during the period when Amendment 2 was passed. The center had always struggled financially, and funding became even scarcer as donors prioritized efforts to overturn Amendment 2. Morgan was among those who kept the organization going through hard times. (Courtesy of Kat Morgan.)

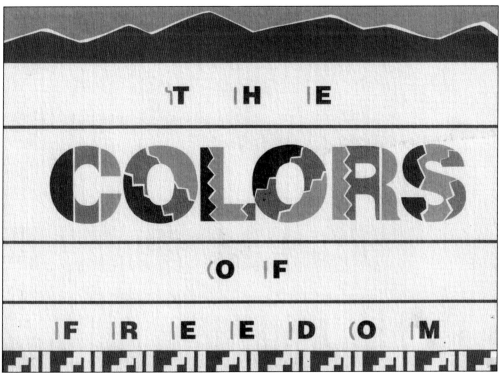

DENVER HUMAN RIGHTS CAMPAIGN DINNER. Even before Amendment 2 passed, Colorado LGBTQ political activists began recognizing the need to support gay rights protections at the federal level. "The Colors of Freedom" was the theme of the first Denver Human Rights Campaign Fund (later renamed HRC) Dinner, held on Saturday, February 1, 1992, at the Westin Hotel Tabor Center with a price of $150 per person. Colorado's inaugural fundraiser for the national organization was cochaired by Julia Fitz-Randolph and Lee Rudofsky, and honorary cochairs were Congresswoman Patricia Schroeder and Mayor Wellington Webb. (Courtesy of Phil Nash.)

HRC DINNER INTRODUCES AWARD, 1993. Tom Buche (left) and Linda Elliott cochaired the 1993 HRC Denver Dinner, which introduced the annual Paul Hunter Award. The award was given to recognize individuals who exemplify the spirit of Paul Hunter by working tirelessly for social justice, equality, and visibility of the LGBTQ community in Colorado. Paul Hunter Award recipients over the years include Joe Barrows, Jean Hodges, Wayne Jakino, Donaciano Martinez, Jim McNulty, Phil Nash, Morris Price, Karla Rikansrud, Pat Steadman, Faye Tate, and Carol White. (Photograph by David Ford.)

CENTER THRIVES WITH NEW LEADER. The prolonged political crisis that Amendment 2 thrust on Colorado's LGBTQ community sidelined other pressing priorities. The Gay and Lesbian Community Center nearly folded in 1995, kept alive by a handful of board members and volunteers. In 1997, the center's board hired Mike Smith, a cofounder and leader of the NAMES Project (AIDS Quilt), to turn the organization around. Under Smith's leadership, over the next four years, the budget increased nearly tenfold, staffing levels reached an all-time high, and the annual Pride celebration became the sixth largest in the United States. (Photograph by Phil Nash.)

EQUALITY COLORADO BUILDS STATEWIDE NETWORK. In the late 1990s, Sue Anderson (left), who served as executive director of the Gay and Lesbian Community Center in the early 1990s, headed Equality Colorado, a new statewide organization to build grassroots support for LGBTQ rights, a pressing need given the electoral success of the Amendment 2 ballot initiative in 1992. Pictured with Anderson at PrideFest 1999 are Phyllis Lyon (right) and Del Martin, life partners and cofounders, in the early 1950s, of the Daughters of Bilitis, the nation's first lesbian organization. Martin and Lyons were grand marshals for that year's Pride parade. (Courtesy of Sue Anderson.)

Eight

MARCHING INTO THE MAINSTREAM

The 1980s and the first half of the 1990s were traumatic for LGBTQ people nationally and in Colorado. In 1995, fourteen years after the first AIDS patients were reported, effective antiviral therapies began turning the tide, reducing deaths from HIV/AIDS from 1996 on. By then, more than 250,000 Americans had died, making AIDS the leading cause of death for people 25–44. In Colorado, the trauma was compounded by the 1992 passage of Amendment 2, with no resolution until 1996 when it was ruled unconstitutional, leaving LGBTQ Coloradans in suspense about whether they would be permanently relegated to second-class citizenship. Another crushing blow came on October 7, 1998, when 21-year-old University of Wyoming student Matthew Shepard was found brutally beaten and left for dead in a field near Laramie. His death six days later in a Fort Collins hospital ignited candlelight vigils and angry rallies nationwide, bringing a laser focus to anti-LGBTQ violence and demands for hate crimes legislation.

The Amendment 2 victory at the US Supreme Court cemented the resolve among LGBTQ people to become visible and mighty forces in politics, business, medicine, law, religion, and the media—every part of the social structure that had, for generations, contributed to their oppression and stigmatization. Denverite Jennifer Veiga became the first openly lesbian state legislator, first elected in 1997 and coming out publicly in 2002 during her successful reelection campaign. In 2000, open lesbian attorney Mary Celeste, who helped mount the legal challenge to Amendment 2, was appointed a Denver county judge by Mayor Wellington Webb, serving until 2015. As the new millennium dawned, many Denver congregations began displaying rainbow banners signaling an "open and affirming" welcome to LGBTQ worshipers. Popular TV host Chris Parente never hid his gay orientation as he climbed the ranks to rise to media prominence. Each year's Pride parade included new corporate LGBTQ employee resource groups representing financial services, airlines, retailers, technology companies, the automotive and hospitality industries, and more.

Since 2010, the LGBTQ advocacy organization One Colorado (OC) has led the charge to advance pro-LGBTQ legislation. OC has scored victories during most legislative sessions, aided by a growing number of out LGBTQ legislators and allies. In 2018, Coloradans elected Jared Polis to the state's highest office, making him the nation's first openly gay male governor and his husband, Marlon Reis, the nation's first first gentleman. Polis was reelected in 2022 and is often mentioned as a future presidential candidate.

MAYOR WELLINGTON WEBB, SERVED 1991–2003. In 1991, Denver voters elected Wellington Webb, left, the city's first Black mayor, pictured here in 1993. Webb was first elected to the Colorado House of Representatives in 1972 and later served in top-appointed roles in both federal and state agencies, followed by serving one term as Denver's elected auditor from 1987 to 1991. Webb, along with his wife, Wilma Webb, were among the earliest gay rights supporters in the state, with Webb cosponsoring gay antidiscrimination legislation in 1975. Webb formed Denver's first LGBTQ Commission, an advisory body now embedded in Denver's governing fabric. (Photograph by David Ford.)

QUEER YOUTH MARCH IN WASHINGTON. Rainbow Alley is the Center on Colfax's program for LGBTQ youth, established in the late 1990s with partial startup funding from the City of Denver. In April 2000, several Rainbow Alley participants took part in the Millennium March on Washington to raise awareness and visibility of LGBTQ Americans. Julie Voyles (left), then the center's director of youth services, accompanied Rainbow Alley's delegation to the march. (Photograph by Bill Olson.)

WELCOME TO THE FORCE. On March 24, 2000, Denver Police Department (DPD) chief Gerry Whitman shakes hands with newly graduated police officer Kevin Malloy, the first known gay man who was out when he applied to join the DPD. A decade earlier, Malloy had worked with the Equal Protection Ordinance Coalition, which successfully advocated with the Denver City Council to pass a comprehensive human rights ordinance to extend anti-discrimination protections based on sexual orientation. (Transgender protections were added later.) Later promoted to corporal, Malloy, who rejected the term "gay cop," spent the bulk of his career as a field training officer. (Courtesy of Kevin Malloy.)

DON'T ASK, DON'T TELL. At the beginning of the 21st century, LGB people could avoid being discharged from the US military if they were able to keep their sexual orientation secret but could be discharged if they came out. But proud veterans had no reason to observe the policy. Clark Thompson, pictured here in the 2000 Denver Pride parade, achieved the rank of lieutenant commander in the US Navy. During his retirement from the Navy, he owned two Denver gay bars, the Triangle Lounge (1998–2005) and the Den (2001–2005). (Photograph by Phil Nash.)

JUDGE MARY CELESTE SWORN IN. In 2000, Mayor Wellington Webb (right) appointed Mary Celeste (center) to serve as a Denver County judge, the first open LGBTQ person named to the Denver bench. She is pictured being sworn in by Judge Raymond Sattler. Serving until 2015, Judge Celeste was also the first woman and first LGBTQ person to serve as the presiding judge, a role she assumed in 2010. Celeste had earlier cofounded and helped lead the Colorado Legal Initiatives Project, which worked to get Amendment 2 declared unconstitutional. (Courtesy of Mary Celeste.)

OUTGIVING BOOSTS LGBTQ PHILANTHROPY. Tech entrepreneur and philanthropist Tim Gill speaks at a 2003 Outgiving Conference hosted by the Gill Foundation. Since 1996, the Gill Foundation has hosted private biennial conferences that invite donors who give $25,000-plus annually to network with each other and learn about opportunities for collaboration with like-minded funders to increase the effectiveness and impact of their philanthropic giving in support of LGBTQ equality. (Courtesy of the Gill Foundation.)

CONGRESSWOMAN DIANA DEGETTE AND MORRIS PRICE. DeGette, a Democrat, was first elected to represent Colorado Congressional District 1 in 1996, succeeding Pat Schroeder, who held the office for 24 years. With DeGette is Morris Price, her district director from 2010 to 2015. Price, who formerly worked for the University of Denver, the Gill Foundation, and City Year, has held numerous volunteer and professional leadership roles in the Denver community and LGBTQ organizations. (Courtesy of Morris Price.)

A HOME OF ITS OWN. On September 17, 2010, almost 34 years after its founding, the Gay, Lesbian, Bisexual, and Transgender Community Center fulfilled a long-held dream by opening the doors of the first building it ever owned. In this photograph, visitors line up for their first glimpse of the new facility. Now known as the Center on Colfax, the building was more than an asset for the LGBTQ community; it also helped improve and invigorate a key section of the often-gritty East Colfax corridor. (Photograph by Stevie Creselius, courtesy of the Center on Colfax.)

THE NEW CENTER'S GRAND OPENING. CEO Carlos Martinez welcomes guests at the grand opening festivities held on the Center on Colfax's rooftop, a unique feature with city and mountain views used frequently for social gatherings and the annual PrideFest viewing platform. Martinez led a three-year, $3-million capital campaign to purchase and renovate a blighted former bank building at 1301 East Colfax Avenue, just a half-block from the center's first office at 1436 Lafayette Street. Martinez left the center in 2013 to become the CEO of the Latino Community Foundation of Colorado. He was succeeded by Debra Pollock. (Photograph by Stevie Creselius, courtesy of the Center on Colfax.)

BEQUEST ANCHORS CENTER'S CAPITAL CAMPAIGN. Volunteer Roy G. Wood was generally a quiet person who did not focus a lot of attention on himself while he was helping out around the Center on Colfax nearly every day, spending most of his time in the center's library. Much to the surprise of center staff, Wood left the Center on Colfax $1.2 million in his will when he died in 2007. The magnitude of the gift made it possible to create a capital campaign to raise another nearly $2 million to purchase and renovate 1301 East Colfax Avenue. (Courtesy of the Center on Colfax.)

SHE RAN THE SHOW. Debra Pollock, left, pictured at PrideFest in 2016 with her wife, Maureen Anderson, served as the CEO of the Center on Colfax from 2014 to 2019, promoted from her previous role as vice president of development and communications since 2004. During her tenure, Pollock oversaw a $3-million capital campaign to buy and remodel a headquarters for the center and, in 2009, helped to expand PrideFest to a two-day event as attendance grew to hundreds of thousands. (Photograph by Stevie Crecelius, courtesy of Debra Pollock.)

HE RAN THE PARADE. Anthony Aragon (right) volunteered to coordinate Denver's Pride parade in the late 1990s and served in that role for 19 consecutive years. Travis Jensen (left) assisted him for many of those years. Aragon's drag persona, Lushus La'Rell, was elected the fortieth Empress of the Imperial Court of the Rocky Mountain Empire and has raised tens of thousands of dollars for both LGBTQ and mainstream charities. During his career, Aragon has worked for several Denver mayors and one governor. (Courtesy of David Westman.)

FIRST LGBTQ SENATE MINORITY LEADER. Sen. Lucía Guzmán (left) represented a northwest Denver district in the state senate from 2010 to 2019. A Democrat, Guzmán was the first Hispanic and first open lesbian to become senate minority leader, a role she held until 2018. Before serving in the senate, Guzmán served on the Denver Public Schools Board of Education from 1999 to 2007. An ordained Methodist minister, Guzmán headed the Colorado Council of Churches from 1994 to 1999. This 2011 photograph pictures her taking part in the Girls with Goals program at the state capitol. (Courtesy of Colorado Senate Democrats.)

FIRST LGBTQ CITY COUNCIL MEMBER. In 2011, councilwoman at large Robin Kniech was the first out LGBTQ person elected to Denver City Council, where she served three four-year terms, thus becoming the longest-serving LGBTQ elected official in Colorado when she was term-limited in 2023. An attorney, wife, and mother, Kniech advocated for several pro-LGBTQ policies as well as for economic and social justice issues. She was especially known for her leadership on affordable housing, livable wages, and humane treatment of homeless persons and undocumented immigrants. (Courtesy of Robin Kniech.)

THUMBS UP FOR CIVIL UNIONS. On March 21, 2013, Gov. John Hickenlooper (seated) signed Colorado's civil unions bill, making Colorado the ninth state in the nation to grant legal rights similar to marriage. Flanking the governor are five of the eight openly LGBTQ legislators serving in 2013: from left to right, Joann Ginal, Mark Ferrandino, Sue Schaefer, an unidentified woman, Pat Steadman (the bill's lead sponsor), and Paul Rosenthal. In 2014, a court decision made same-sex marriage legal in Colorado, and on June 26, 2015, the US Supreme Court decision in *Obergefell v. Hodges* legalized same-sex marriage in all 50 states. (Photograph by James S. Peterson, courtesy of History Colorado.)

SIMONS FIRST TO MARRY. Long-term partners Anna Sher Simon (left) and Fran Simon were ready when an October 6, 2014, court ruling removed legal barriers to same-sex marriage in Colorado. Already the first same-sex Colorado couple to obtain a legal civil union, they were the first same-sex couple to get a marriage license the day after the court ruling. When they learned the Denver city clerk would start issuing marriage licenses, they donned wedding gowns and got married at city hall. The "just married" couple appeared at an October 8, 2014, rally at Denver's federal courthouse. (Photograph by Matthew Staver, courtesy of the Gill Foundation.)

Huge Wedding Cake Celebrates Gay Marriage. Same-sex marriage became legal in Colorado on October 7, 2014. Denver PrideFest organizers commissioned artist Lonnie Hanzon to create a giant wedding cake to celebrate this historic milestone at the Pride celebration the following June. Just a few days after the event, on June 26, 2015, the US Supreme Court ruled that same-sex marriage was legal everywhere in the nation. (Photograph by Phil Nash.)

PrideFest Expands to Two Days. From 1976 until 2009, PrideFest was a one-day outdoor event at Civic Center Park on a Sunday in late June. Recognizing the growing number of LGBTQ-headed families who were attending PrideFest, organizers at the GLBT Center decided to expand the event to a two-day event in 2009, with Saturdays focusing on activities that were more tailored to families and youth and providing family-friendly areas to gather. These dads and at least one of their kids approve of the change. (Photograph by Stevie Creselius, courtesy of the Center on Colfax.)

107

PIONEER GAY LEGISLATOR. Sen. Pat Steadman (left) receives the 2017 One Colorado (OC) Lifetime Achievement Award from OC's then-CEO Daniel Ramos. A lawyer and former lobbyist, Steadman was one of the state's first openly gay legislators, representing Central Denver in the Senate from 2009 to 2017 and championing the successful Civil Unions Act in 2013. As a young law school graduate, Steadman became immersed in politics during the 1992 campaign against Amendment 2 and worked as a lobbyist before running for office. Ramos worked at One Colorado for nine years and was its CEO from 2016 to 2020. (Courtesy of One Colorado.)

TRANSGENDER SPACE ENGINEER. In 2019, One Colorado awarded its Lifetime Achievement Award to Christine Bland (left), an aerospace electrical engineer at Lockheed Martin. After deciding to transition nearly a decade earlier, Bland faced potential consequences as to how it would go over at work; she received strong support from her employer. Pictured with Bland is transgender activist Clemmie Engle, retired from more than 30 years with the state attorney general's office. Engle was once named Barrister of the Year at the GLBT Center's annual Jokers, Jewels, and Justice fundraising event for its legal services program. (Photograph by T.J. Romero, courtesy of One Colorado.)

LOBBY DAY WAKE-UP CALL. Gov. Jared Polis, accompanied by his dog Gia, rallies the citizen lobbyists at the state capitol in Denver on the morning of One Colorado's 2023 Lobby Day. Once called the "hate state" for passing an anti-gay constitutional amendment in 1992, three decades later, Colorado ranks among the nation's most LGBTQ-friendly states. (Courtesy of One Colorado.)

CIVICS 101. No one is ever too young to learn firsthand how government works, how laws are passed, how to make their voices heard, and where to find their elected representatives. These young adults at the state capitol are the faces of a new generation of LGBTQ+ voters and possible future political leaders, and they are learning how to advocate for their rights and the needs of their generation. (Courtesy of One Colorado.)

MARLO'S LAW PROTECTS FAMILIES. House majority leader Daneya Esgar (center) championed a 2022 law to ensure that all parents who conceive through assisted reproductive technology, regardless of gender identity, sexual orientation, or marital status, are eligible for the same rights and legal protections. On the left is Daneya's wife, Heather Palm, holding their daughter Marlo, for whom the law was named. One Colorado Policy director Meredith Gleitz is on the right. (Courtesy of One Colorado.)

GAY HISTORIAN HONORED. In 2023, David Duffield (right) received the Denver Public Library's prestigious Eleanor Gehres Award at a ceremony held at the Center on Colfax, where he directs the LGBTQ History Project. Duffield was recognized for procuring historic documents for the Denver Public Library's archives from dozens of LGBTQ donors, recording more than 100 oral histories, and working to ensure that LGBTQ history is preserved and accessible. "It's about the legacy of the work and making sure that no queer kid ever has to grow up with the same kind of ignorance I've had to grow up with," said Duffield of the honor. (Photograph by Phil Nash.)

Nine

MILESTONES, MEMORIES, AND MOVING FORWARD

Denver's LGBTQ history can be divided into two eras: the hidden history, which came mostly before 1970, and the visible history in the post-Stonewall era, when creative and courageous LGBTQ people were freer to come out and take charge of their destiny. The growth and maturation of Denver's LGBTQ community have come in waves. This book's previous chapters document a succession of stages LGBTQ Denver has passed through to build the open, thriving, and welcoming community of the early 21st century.

This final chapter is devoted to organizations, events, activities, and people who do not fit neatly into the chronological narrative but deserve acknowledgment for their unique, durable, promising, or simply unclassifiable contributions. This includes people who are making history that future generations will read and write about. This chapter salutes organizations that started with a powerful idea—or a glittering dream—and have become anchor institutions in Denver's LGBTQ culture. These pages also pay tribute to ephemeral fragments of Denver's LGBTQ history that mattered for a while and then faded away.

LGBTQ Denver is not the definitive word; there is much more history to reveal and present. Much history needs deeper research and more thorough interpretation. There is much more to learn about the deliberate and cruel suppression of LGBTQ culture, the destruction of individuals' stories, and the forces across generations—even now—that have worked to distort society's perspectives about the existence, accomplishments, triumphs, and tribulations of our LGBTQ predecessors.

Denver is fortunate to have a thriving LGBTQ History Project at the Center on Colfax working with other institutions to collect, preserve, display, and make available for research LGBTQ-related documents and artifacts. These efforts depend on individuals and organizations to contribute their stories, pictures, and documents. Queer people of many varieties have existed throughout history everywhere on the planet. How they have been received ranges from honor and respect to indifference to being despised and ostracized. For most of American history, sexual and gender minorities have been outcasts. Through the hard work of many people beginning in the second half of the 20th century, LGBTQ people have been able to emerge from the shadows to seek justice, equality, freedom, and opportunities to contribute to society without being compelled to hide how they live and love. It is critical to securely embed LGBTQ history into the larger historical narrative so this bountiful heritage offers future generations a source of pride, power, and peace of mind.

SHATTERING THE GAY CEILING. Colorado governor Jared Polis (born 1975) has broken many barriers. An entrepreneur while in college, he became a multimillionaire in his 20s by launching and then selling several internet-based businesses. In 2008, voters in Colorado's liberal 2nd House District elected him the first nonincumbent openly gay man to Congress, and he was re-elected four times and was the first openly gay parent in Congress. Elected governor in 2018, he was the first gay male governor in the United States and the first Jewish governor of Colorado. Polis was overwhelmingly re-elected in 2022. In this photograph, Polis speaks at One Colorado's 2023 Pink Party. (Courtesy of One Colorado.)

SAME-SEX MARRIAGE REACHES COLORADO. In the 1990s, Republican legislators attempted several times to pass a state constitutional amendment banning same-sex marriage. Democratic governor Roy Romer vetoed the legislation. But in 2000, Republican governor Bill Owens signed the constitutional ban. In 2014, a series of court rulings overturned the ban, and on October 6, 2014, the US Supreme Court declined to hear appeals, leading to the ban being lifted the next day. In this photograph, philanthropist Tim Gill speaks at an October 8, 2014, celebratory rally at the US federal courthouse. The Gill Foundation financially supported a variety of initiatives leading to the legal victory. (Courtesy of the Gill Foundation.)

BABES AROUND DENVER. In the fall of 2002, a group of lesbians began discussing a regular happy hour, a challenge because lesbians lacked gathering places. Babes Around Denver (BAD) founder Dede Frain sent an email invitation to her large network for a "December Happy Hour," and by March 2003, the popular "First Friday" dance parties were underway. Twenty years later, BAD has attracted more than 300,000 guest visits. BAD's other signature event is the Official Women's Pride Party, drawing 2,000 or more guests. Pictured are Dede Frain (right) and her wife, Karyl Aidin. (Photograph by Monica Lloyd.)

BAD FUN ON FIRST FRIDAY. Babes Around Denver's "First Friday" events at Tracks night club is the largest and longest-running monthly women's party in the United States. Babes Around Denver attracts women of all ages and backgrounds. "Thousands of women have made new friends, many have entered new relationships, and some have even started new businesses as a result of connections made at First Friday," says founder Dede Frain. BAD is an annual sponsor of PrideFest and donates to LGBTQ charities. (Photograph by Monica Lloyd.)

NUCLIA WASTE IS THE BOMB. In the early 2000s, David Westman created the colorful alter-ego Nuclia Waste, "the triple-nipple queen of comedy." Nuclia navigated many Denver Pride events on stilts, towering over the festivities with mirth and style. Nuclia's favorite saying is "It's never too late to have a happy childhood." (Courtesy of David Westman.)

EL PORTRERO PRIDE FLOAT. El Portrero is an LGBTQ nightclub in Glendale for the Spanish-speaking community. Every year, El Portrero goes all out to dazzle Pride crowds with its Hispanic-themed floats and extravagant costumes reflecting Latin American cultural themes. The Latin Stage at PrideFest is a popular attraction featuring DJs and performances of Spanish-language music. (Photograph by Phil Nash.)

RUPAUL DRAG RACE WINNER. Yvie Oddly is the drag persona of Denver native Jovan Jordan Bridges, who won the 2019 season of *RuPaul's Drag Race* and later competed in *RuPaul Drag Race All Stars*. Before achieving national fame, Oddly performed at Denver PrideFest and Drag Nation at Tracks. Oddly is noted for eccentric and conceptual looks, performance ability, and quirky personality. "If you have a lot of money and you wear something really sparkly . . . the general public is going to fall in love with you," says Oddly. "I wanted to shake that up and remind people that this . . . is a queer art form." (Photograph by Monica Lloyd.)

MAKE ROOM FOR DRAG KINGS. Trans man entertainer Dustin "Pop Pop" Schlong, winner of Mr. Trans Colorado 2023, is a Colorado native who got interested in drag as a teenager in Highlands Ranch. A drag king is usually a female who performs in male attire, but since transitioning to being male, Schlong is the rare drag king who is a man. "As a drag king, we are not seen the same way as drag queens," Schlong told gaydenver.com in a 2022 interview. "As a trans man, advocating for trans people and their rights is incredibly important to me." (Photograph by Monica Lloyd.)

GRASSROOTS ACTIVIST TO FOUNDATION PRESIDENT. Native Iowan Brad Clark (right) helped organize his state's successful campaign for same-sex marriage in the late 2000s. In 2010, he became the founding executive director of One Colorado, leading the organization's statewide push for LGBTQ equality. He joined the Gill Foundation as vice president in 2015 and became president and CEO, leading its mission of securing full equality for all LGBTQ Americans. Clark is pictured with political communications strategist Nico Delgado at OC's 2023 Pink Party. (Courtesy of One Colorado.)

ONE COLORADO CHAMPIONS LGBTQ RIGHTS. One Colorado is the state's leading advocacy organization dedicated to advancing equality for LGBTQ Coloradans and their families. Nadine Bridges was named OC's executive director in January 2021. Trained as a social worker, Bridges leads a team of about a dozen people who advance equity and freedom for LGBTQ Coloradans through state policy, advocacy, health care, and education. She previously served as youth services director at the Center on Colfax and is an adjunct professor at the University of Denver Graduate School of Social Work. (Courtesy of One Colorado.)

CORPORATE VISIBILITY AT PRIDE. USBank is among the scores of corporations and businesses that march in Denver's Pride marches each year. Officially named the Coors Light Denver Pride Parade since the late 1990s, the annual parade is a way for LGBTQ employees of corporations and businesses to boost their employers' image by supporting pro-LGBTQ policies and corporate philanthropy for LGBTQ organizations. Such demonstrations of corporate support were inconceivable in Denver until the late 1990s but now include giants like United Airlines, Starbucks, Verizon, Xfinity, Nissan, and dozens more. (Photograph by Phil Nash.)

ACTIVISTS DENOUNCE CORPORATIONS AT PRIDE. Some LGBTQ political activists oppose corporate participation at Denver's PrideFest, believing that it detracts from the original intent of Pride marches as acts of protest. "We are not represented by Coors. We are not represented by all these corporations that are here at Pride today," said Lucas Evans, lead organizer of the Rise Up Trans Rights protest, to *Denverite* in June 2023. PrideFest organizers respond by emphasizing how corporate funding at Pride supports programs and services year-round at the Center on Colfax, PrideFest's producer. (Photograph by Katie Bush, courtesy of History Colorado.)

2016 Pride Honors Pulse Victims. The deadly massacre at Orlando's Pulse nightclub that killed 49 patrons and wounded 53 others—most of them LGBTQ Latinos—was fresh in the minds of Denver PrideFest attendees in 2016. Artist Lonnie Hanzen created a large black box to commemorate the deadliest mass shooting in US history up to that time, and Pride attendees wrote messages in rainbow-colored chalk. (Photograph by Phil Nash.)

Black Trans Lives Matter. Anti-racism demonstrations erupted across the nation in 2020 as protesters enraged at police brutality that led to the death of George Floyd took to the streets to demand justice. Recognizing that Black trans women are among the most vulnerable to violent victimization, a group called the Pride Liberation March united with Black Lives Matter 5280 in June 2020 to hold a rally in Cheesman Park and march to Civic Center Park. Pictured are four Black trans women who took part in the protest. (Photograph by Thomas Elliott.)

2023 PRIDE HONORS SHOOTING SURVIVORS. On November 19, 2022, a shooter armed with an AR-15 style firearm entered Club Q, a popular Colorado Springs gay bar, and started shooting randomly into the crowd, killing five people; 19 others sustained nonfatal gunshot wounds, and additional victims were injured in other ways. Survivors of the Club Q shooting were invited to serve as grand marshals of the 2023 Pride parade in Denver. In June 2023, the shooter pled guilty and was sentenced to five consecutive life terms in prison without possibility of parole plus 2,211 years. (Photograph by Phil Nash.)

POLICE READY TO DEFEND PRIDE. In 2023, with a precipitous nationwide rise in anti-LGBTQ rhetoric and violence directed primarily at transgender people, the Denver Police Department deployed heavily armed tactical units to go into action if necessary at the 2023 Pride parade. While no threats were reported, the fresh memory of a shooter entering Club Q in Colorado Springs on November 19, 2022, leaving five people dead and 25 injured weighed heavily on the minds of many. While some activists protest the presence of police at Pride events, ultimately it is their job to keep the public safe. (Photograph by Phil Nash.)

LEGACY FOR **LGBTQ** MENTAL HEALTH. In 2023, the Center on Colfax opened Glass Lawler Mental Health, a program that provides free therapeutic counseling and peer support for LGBTQ individuals. The program is named for benefactors Kathy Glass (1932–2014, pictured above) and Carmah Lawler (1929–2020), a married lesbian couple who were together for more than 30 years before Kathy's death. Both had worked professionally as social workers, were involved in social justice political activities, and belonged to Older Lesbians Organizing for Change (OLOC), a group for lesbians over 55 offering support, engagement, and opportunities to advance social justice. (Both, courtesy of OLOC Archive.)

ROOFTOP PRIDE. Rex Fuller, CEO of the Center on Colfax since 2019, speaks to a donor gathering on the center's rooftop. The murals behind him, by artist Gina Franco, depict Sylvia Rivera, left, and Marcia P. Johnson, gender-nonconforming activists who were involved in the 1969 Stonewall uprising and subsequent activism for LGBTQ liberation and equality. (Photograph by Phil Nash.)

LESBIAN BAR AMONG NATION'S FEW. Opened in 2013, Blush 'N Blu, at 1526 East Colfax Avenue, is one of the few remaining lesbian bars in North America and the only one in Denver. Describing itself as "a warm and casual queer-inclusive bar in the center of Denver," Blush 'N Blu's motto is, "All are welcome, intolerance is not." The popular bar attracts a diverse clientele offering a variety of entertainments including karaoke, game nights, open-mic poetry and music, and live entertainment. In this photograph, Blush 'N Blu patrons line dance while waiting for the 2023 Pride parade to pass by. (Photograph by Phil Nash.)

IMPERIAL COURT GOLDEN ANNIVERSARY. Founded in 1973, the Imperial Court of the Rocky Mountain Empire (ICRME) is the longest-surviving nonreligious LGBTQ organization in Colorado, here pictured in a 50th-anniversary group portrait of the College of Monarchs, its surviving leaders. ICRME is part of the International Imperial Court System, which originated in San Francisco in the mid-1960s, and has grown to become the second-largest LGBTQ organization in the world, surpassed only by the Metropolitan Community Church. The court system is a grassroots network of local and regional organizations that builds community relationships and raises money for charitable causes. ICRME's signature event is its annual Coronation ball, where the newly elected Emperor and Empress are installed to lead the organization in the following year. ICRME's first coronation

in 1974 was held in a Denver VFW hall, but the gala soon moved to the grand ballroom of the Downtown Denver Hilton and then on to other large ballrooms that can accommodate 1,000 or more guests. Coronation attracts Imperial Court royalty from around the nation, and Denver's monarchs travel to other cities as ambassadors. Over the decades, ICRME members have staged hundreds of events raising millions of dollars for charities in the LGBTQ community, HIV/AIDS organizations, and mainstream groups. Established in 1994, ICRME's White Rose Scholarship Foundation annually provides about $15,000 in funds to support tuition and textbook costs for Colorado residents pursuing higher education. (Photograph by Snap Shots Photography Studio, courtesy of Annie Brenman-West.)

COMING OUT, MARRYING AT 90-SOMETHING. Kenneth Felts (right) made headlines when he came out on Facebook in 2020 at the age of 90, and he made headlines again in 2023 when he married 34-year-old Johnny Hau (left). A Korean War veteran, Felts had a secret love affair with a man when he was young, but feelings of religious guilt drove him away. He later married a woman and had a daughter who, herself, came out as a lesbian decades ago, even as Felts remained closeted until regrets over his long-ago gay love affair emerged during COVID-19 isolation. (Courtesy of Kenneth Felts.)

JUDE'S LAW EASES GENDER CHANGE. In 2019, the Colorado legislature passed Jude's Law to simplify the process for legal name changes and gender marker corrections on identity documents and birth certificates. Representative Brianna Titone (left), the first transgender person elected to the Colorado General Assembly, poses with Jude, then an eighth-grade student who testified four years in a row in support of the bill. Jude's Law provides the options of F, M, or X on IDs and birth certificates and removes the requirements of surgery, a doctor's note, a court order, and newspaper publication to make changes. (Courtesy of One Colorado.)

COUNCIL MEMBERS TAKE OATH. In the spring of 2023, voters elected Shontel Lewis (left, facing forward), Denver's first Black lesbian city council member, and Darrell Watson (right), Denver's first out gay male council member, shown here being sworn in on July 17, 2023. The mother of two sons, Lewis describes herself as "an unapologetic, Black, Queer Womxn." Representing District 8 in Northwest Denver, Lewis previously served on the elected board of the Regional Transportation District, worked as a vice president with the Colorado Coalition for the Homeless, and earlier led family and community engagement activities at Denver Public Schools. Formerly employed in the financial services industry, Watson represents District 10 in north central Denver. Prior to being elected, Watson served in many civic volunteer and leadership roles within Denver city government in diverse areas including housing, policing, and parks and recreation. Watson is married to Mike Wenk, who is also his business partner in the Watson Wenk Group consulting firm. (Photograph by Evan Semón, courtesy of Darrell Watson.)

PAUL HUNTER (1942–1991). Attorney Paul Hunter was a prominent gay rights activist who, as a young attorney, got involved with the Gay Coalition of Denver and the Lesbian/Gay Legal Workers. He also served on the board of the Gay and Lesbian Community Center and helped mobilize LGBTQ support to elect Mayor Federico Peña in 1983. After his death from AIDS, the Human Rights Campaign Colorado Steering Committee named an award in his honor to be given annually to individuals who "exemplify the spirit of Paul Hunter by working tirelessly for social justice, equality and visibility of the LGBT community." (Courtesy of Phil Nash.)

ELLIS MCFADDEN (1949–2015). Throughout his adult life, Ellis McFadden exemplified the spirit of volunteerism in Denver's LGBTQ community. Although he was not wealthy, he gave as generously as he could to LGBTQ nonprofit and political organizations. He was an early supporter of the Gay Community Center, a founding member of the Denver Gay Men's Chorus, and a perennial canvasser for Democratic candidates for office. When he died, hundreds attended his memorial service at Project Angel Heart, where he was a meal-delivery volunteer. Before his death, Gov. John Hickenlooper and the legislature honored McFadden for his community service. (Photograph by Phil Nash.)

A MESSAGE FOR ALL TIME. "Love is love," the dominant theme of PrideFest 2023, is a simple but powerful message to disrupt the traditional and deeply ingrained view that only cisgender heterosexual people can—or may—experience love in their lives. The oppression of LGBTQ people depends on the perpetuation of a binary values system, rooted in religious codes, that stigmatizes and punishes sexual and/or gender variation. For more than a half-century, out and proud LGBTQ activists have successfully chipped away at legal, medical, and social barriers, paving the way for current and future generations to live and love free from shame and scorn. As history has shown at other times and in other places, victories for social justice can be overcome and progress can be erased. The challenge of the future is to protect the freedoms that have been achieved while building an inclusive LGBTQ culture based on truth, justice, compassion, and yes—love. (Photograph by Phil Nash.)

DISCOVER THOUSANDS OF LOCAL HISTORY BOOKS
FEATURING MILLIONS OF VINTAGE IMAGES

Arcadia Publishing, the leading local history publisher in the United States, is committed to making history accessible and meaningful through publishing books that celebrate and preserve the heritage of America's people and places.

Find more books like this at
www.arcadiapublishing.com

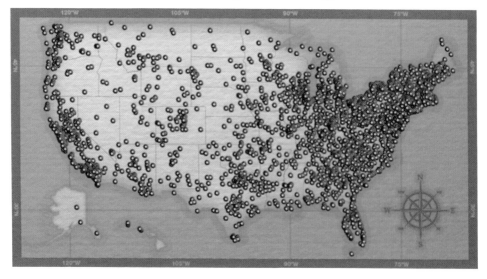

Search for your hometown history, your old stomping grounds, and even your favorite sports team.

Consistent with our mission to preserve history on a local level, this book was printed in South Carolina on American-made paper and manufactured entirely in the United States. Products carrying the accredited Forest Stewardship Council (FSC) label are printed on 100 percent FSC-certified paper.

MADE IN THE